Compensating the Sales Force

Compensating the Sales Force

A Practical Guide to Designing Winning Sales Reward Programs

Second Edition

David J. Cichelli

New York   Chicago   San Francisco   Lisbon   London
Madrid   Mexico City   Milan   New Delhi   San Juan
Seoul   Singapore   Sydney   Toronto

The **McGraw·Hill** Companies

1 2 3 4 5 6 7 8 9 0   WFR/WFR   1 9 8 7 6 5 4 3 2 1 0

ISBN: 978-0-07-173902-3
MHID: 0-07-173902-5

This publication is designed to provide accurate and authoritative information in regard to the subject matter covered. It is sold with the understanding that neither the author or the publisher is engaged in rendering legal, accounting, or other professional service. If legal advice or other expert assistance is required, the services of a competent professional person should be sought.

> —*From a Declaration of Principles Jointly Adopted by a Committee of the American Bar Association and a Committee of Publishers and Associations*

McGraw-Hill books are available at special quantity discounts to use as premiums and sales promotions, or for use in corporate training programs. To contact a representative, please visit the Contact Us pages at www.mhprofessional.com.

This book is printed on acid-free paper.

To Mario and Genevieve Cichelli

Contents

Acknowledgments

Sales compensation affects tens of thousands, perhaps hundreds of thousands, of sales personnel on a worldwide basis who work with driven enthusiasm on behalf of their employers. Sales management professionals strive to create win-win opportunities for both sales personnel and their companies. It's been my pleasure to work with—and learn from—exceptional sales management leaders, who have helped me test and retest the sales compensation principles you will find in this book. I thank all of my clients who have contributed to building this emerging body of knowledge.

And I extend my special thanks to WorldatWork, which has supported my work over the years, allowing me to create, modify, and improve sales compensation courses now taught to thousands of compensation and sales professionals. Without the opportunity to meet with so many executives in a classroom setting, the material in this book would not have met the test of time or reflect the challenges and suggestions of thousands of students. For this, I am most grateful to the continued support of Anne Ruddy, the Executive Director of WorldatWork. Additionally, WorldatWork has granted me permission to use select charts and concepts from these courses.

My partners at The Alexander Group, Inc.—Gary Tubridy and Robert Conti—continue to provide their unflagging support and encouragement. Also, my fellow consultants never rest as they look for new sales effectiveness solutions to help clients adopt best-of-class sales growth solutions.

And special thanks to Lori Feuer for proofing this second edition.

Finally, to my wife, Kathleen, and daughters Diane and Joan . . . thanks for your loving support.

Preface

Effective sales compensation design is an enduring objective. Since its first publication in 2003, *Compensating the Sales Force* continues to serve general managers, sales executives, sales operations specialists, HR/compensation professionals, finance leaders, and IT support teams. Now published in both the Russian and Chinese languages, the constructs of designing strategically aligned and motivating incentive plans for sales personnel are universal. We continue to teach these concepts to hundreds of executives here in the United States and throughout the world, including Hong Kong, Singapore, Barcelona, Dubai, Cairo, London, Paris, Kuala Lumpur, Bangkok, and many other venues in Europe, Asia, and Latin America. Along with my fellow consultants here at The Alexander Group, Inc., we have the privilege to engage with best thinkers and leaders from worldwide sales organizations as they transform their sales teams to address ever-changing sales challenges. These opportunities to work with clients help us to create cutting-edge and innovative sales growth solutions, including advanced sales compensation methods.

This second edition reflects our most current thinking on sales compensation best practices. Our clients continue to challenge us to create solutions for difficult to compensate sales jobs, complex sales organizations, and global sales teams. We address each of these topics with their own chapter in this second edition of *Compensating the Sales Force*. We have fully reformatted Chapter 5—the "Formula Types" chapter—and we have added new and proven incentive mechanics. If you are accountable for sales compensation design within your company, you can rest assured you have the most complete sales compensation companion in the second edition of *Compensating the Sales Force*.

To learn more, visit these Web sites:
www.compensatingthesalesforce.com
www.salescompsolutions.com
www.alexandergroupinc.com

Introduction

Welcome to the powerful—and sometimes confusing—world of sales compensation!

If you are reading this, you probably work with a sales force and your never-ending objective is to help improve sales performance. Your company might be a manufacturer, service provider, reseller, or retailer; your customers might be other businesses or consumers. Your company might sell direct to end users or through channel partners; your sales force might be small or large.

You know that sales compensation is one of many tools available to help you direct your company's sales efforts. You also know that if done correctly, sales compensation can dramatically improve performance; if done poorly, it can cripple your sales efforts.

Whether you are a sales executive, sales manager, sales operations specialist, finance executive, human resources (HR) compensation manager, information technology (IT) professional, general manager of your division or CEO of your company, you recognize that the goal of increased profitable sales rests squarely with the sales force.

Let's assume you have one of two objectives: You either (1) want to confirm you have a great sales compensation program, or (2) need to develop a new sales compensation plan. This book will provide the answers you seek.

Let's begin:

Sales compensation works!

How salespeople are paid has an immense effect on their performance. With appropriate respect, we will avoid the quagmire of motivational theories that attempt to explain *why* sales compensation works. As any sales manager will attest, salespeople pay very close attention to their sales compensation plan. No, it's not the only reason why sales personnel succeed or fail, but it plays a pivotal role in the overall mix of sales management supervisory tools.

WHY THIS BOOK

Even though sales compensation is a powerful tool, it can be confusing, too. The setting of target pay, selecting the right performance measures, establishing quotas, determining the mix and upside opportunity, and constructing the right formula are examples of the many choices facing those responsible for crafting the right sales compensation plan. The purpose of this book is to guide you through this effort, helping you make the right choices.

Over the years, I have had the pleasure to teach thousands of professionals how to design and implement successful sales compensation plans. I have also enjoyed the support of my clients as we work together to structure effective sales strategies. You will find other sales compensation books that are informative and helpful, particularly in understanding how strategy drives tactics. This book will take your learning to the next level by showing you how to construct effective sales compensation plans. While it will cover numerous technical topics, it will never stray too far from the practicality of this effort: Sales compensation can significantly affect a company's performance. Of course, it affects people's pay, too. Technical or not, it doesn't get much more personal than that!

HOW THIS BOOK IS ORGANIZED

Through the following chapters, you will learn how to construct sales compensation plans that reward sales excellence.

Chapter 1: Why Sales Compensation? Sales compensation helps sales organizations exceed their objectives. However, sales force and sales compensation plans can quickly become outdated. The challenge, as this chapter explains, is to keep the sales compensation plan contemporary with the sales job.

Chapter 2: Sales Compensation Fundamentals. This chapter outlines the basic concepts of sales compensation design. These concepts transcend industries.

Chapter 3: Who Owns Sales Compensation? This chapter explores the process and governance of effective sales compensation.

Chapter 4: Why Job Content Drives Sales Compensation Design. The source of sales compensation design is sales job content—not industry, not legacy solutions, and not management whim. There are well over 40 different types of sales jobs. We examine several jobs to show how sales compensation varies by sales job type.

Chapter 5: Formula Types. In this chapter, you will find the taxonomy of sales compensation formula types. The chapter provides a hierarchy of formula types, terms, and applications.

Chapter 6: Formula Construction. This chapter describes the methods to construct and calculate formulas for payout purposes. You will need a calculator.

Chapter 7: Support Programs: Territories, Quotas, and Crediting. Sales compensation cannot exist without effective support programs such as quota allocation, sales crediting, and account assignment.

Chapter 8: Difficult to Compensate Sales Jobs. There are numerous jobs that present unique sales compensation challenges. This chapter suggests solutions for 13 difficult to compensate jobs.

Chapter 9: Compensating the Complex Sales Organization. Complex sales entities have numerous jobs, challenging crediting issues, and tough measurement conditions. This chapter guides you through these often confounding conditions.

Chapter 10: Global Sales Compensation. Global sales teams are now a fact of life for many sales organizations. In this chapter we sort through which practices should be global and which practices should be local.

Chapter 11: Administration. Good methods to administer sales compensation programs are necessary so the payouts can be made in a timely and accurate manner. Follow the guidelines presented here to ensure you have the right level of support.

Chapter 12: Implementation and Communication. Rolling out the new plan and ongoing communication helps drive perceived equity into the plan.

Chapter 13: Program Assessment. Is it working or not? A lot of money flows through sales compensation programs. This chapter provides the criteria for judging and improving current programs.

Chapter 14: Sales Compensation Design. This chapter provides the how-to step-by-step approach to redesign the sales compensation plans at your company.

Appendix A provides a sample sales compensation plan. **Appendix B** is a list of sales compensation surveys. **Appendix C** provides a list of software vendors.

Compensating
the Sales Force

Chapter 1

Why Sales Compensation?

THE ROLE OF THE SALES FORCE

The role of the sales force is clear. Sell the company's products and services to new and existing customers.

Of course, most of us can easily visualize the "classic" salesperson. Our able and determined salesperson has a geographic territory, travels from one account to another visiting customers and potential buyers, demonstrating the latest gizmo easily drawn from a sample kit or well presented in a glossy brochure. However, this typical image is not fully consistent with today's modern complex sales force. While our fabled territory sales rep is not gone, he or she has been joined by a cadre of sellers. Many companies now sell through multiple sales channels. Our territory rep is now part of a complex customer coverage model that includes telesales, major account sales, product overlay specialists, and partner management. To compound matters, the definition of *products* now varies widely from physical products to services to solutions. To add additional variables, the definition of *sales revenue* has expanded beyond the initial purchase dollars to include rental, lease, product usage revenue, and maintenance revenue.

Further, today's sales organizations are often fully integrated with other formerly disconnected customer contact units such as Customer Service, Contracts, Customer Finance, and Collections. In other words, while the classic sales job still exists for many companies, the territory salesperson traveling from one account to another is just one more member of a much more varied and complex sales coverage system.

For conventional purposes, we will continue to refer to today's sales coverage system as the "sales force," fully recognizing the expanded characteristics of today's sales departments.

Regardless of the complexity of the sales organization, the sales force continues to serve its primary charter of identifying, securing, and servicing customers. The sales department has at the apex of its objectives what no other department has: the responsibility to manage the profitable revenue growth from the company's customers.

WHY SALES COMPENSATION WORKS

Some non-salespeople assume sales representatives are solely money motivated. They believe the best (and only way) to manage the sales force is with an overly lucrative sales compensation program. Of course, this is not true. This monetary-centric view of sales representatives promotes a cursory view and inaccurate assumption about sales representatives. It can lead to some false and unfortunate conclusions about the importance of the sales compensation program.

The source of effective management has many competing theories. While the names and themes of these theories might vary, they all subscribe to at least two critical elements: *leadership communication* and *performance measurement*. Great sales compensation plans optimize both of these elements: communication ("this is what's important") and performance measurement ("your incentive payment for last month's performance"). However, clear communication messages and measurement systems don't always fit tidily into a sales compensation plan. There are other and more powerful ways to manage salespeople. For example, day-to-day, hands-on committed sales supervision is considered the best "system" for optimizing sales performance.

A typical conversation between the first-line supervisor and his or her sales charges would sound something like this: "Now, ladies and gentlemen, we are on the line here to achieve this month's sales objectives. I have a commitment from each of you to reach your monthly quota. It's important to me, and it should be important to you. At our next sales meeting, we will put the numbers up on the board to see who we *cheer* and who we *sneer!* If you are having any trouble closing a deal, I can help you. Call me, and we will schedule joint sales calls. Remember, your success is my success!"

This pitch by the first-line supervisor shows the importance of leadership communication (". . . it's important to me, and it should be important to you . . .") and performance measurement (". . . at our next sales meeting, we will put the numbers up on the board to see who we *cheer* and who we *sneer* . . ."). Notice, no mention of money was made, but a heavy dosage of personal accountability and peer pressure is evident.

Interestingly, this vignette illustrates how sales compensation is considered "cross-elastic" with effective sales management. In other words, the better the sales supervision the less the need for aggressive incentive plans to manage sales performance. Further, sales compensation is not a birthright of salespeople. We estimate that 20 percent of all sales personnel are paid with a salary-only program without any variable pay plan.

Regardless of the pay plan, high-performing sales organizations feature ongoing leadership communication and robust perform-ance measurement systems, whether these functions are found in the sales compensation plan or projected through effective sales management, or are a combination of both.

Yes, we agree, the economic transactional value of the incentive compensation dollars *does* provide motivation for increased performance. However, we consider it complementary to other factors such as pride of performance, supervision, affiliation, and goal accomplishment.

Well-run sales departments treat sales compensation as one of several levers of effective management. Along with other management tools, sales compensation can play a contributing role to successful sales production. However, it cannot be the only factor because alone it cannot provide leadership, commitment, and purpose of endeavor that effective sales management can so ideally provide.

THE POWER OF SALES COMPENSATION

A well-designed sales job and sales compensation program can provide dramatic improvement to a company's sales results. When products, customers, sales leadership, jobs, measures, and rewards are in alignment, sales results can be more than remarkable. Sales compensation can provide the right focus on revenue growth, profit improvement, product focus, account penetration, and solution selling.

If sales compensation programs are so powerful, why do they seem to be so "noisy"? In a league of their own, like no other compensation program that the company has, sales compensation programs seem to produce a disproportionate amount of challenges and conflicts. Why is that? There are several reasons. Some issues are to be expected, but others are a result of poor design and poor alignment. Here are examples of some challenges and conflicts:

1. *The chief executive officer (CEO) and the chief financial officer (CFO) are unhappy that the sales compensation program is too costly while the company is performing below objective.* This is not an

uncommon situation. Before concluding that the sales compensation plan is overpaying, you might want to look at the cost of sales. A high cost of sales might be a result of overstaffing and not overpayment to individuals. If actual payouts are too high, then examine the quota system first. Perhaps quotas are too easy.

2. *Product management wants greater product focus from the sales force.* Product managers want to put extra incentives in the sales compensation plan to promote specific products. Product focus is a legitimate measure for sales compensation purposes; however, prior to making changes, product managers have to make good on their own responsibilities, including rationalizing the product offering, segmenting customers, and providing sales messages for unique buyer populations.

3. *Salespeople complain sales quotas are too difficult.* Sales quotas should be difficult. That's their purpose—to stretch performance. Sales compensation is not an appeasement program.

4. *Salespeople seem to ignore components of the sales compensation program.* This is often the result of a poor sales compensation design, not a motivation issue. A poor design is frequently a reflection of strategy and alignment confusion by senior management. Too many measures, inappropriate measures, or unrealistic objectives will cause sales personnel to ignore one or more components of an incentive plan. Solution: new job definition and a new sales compensation design.

5. *The company spends too much money administering the pay program.* Using low-power tools such as desktop software will cause an increase in headcount for program administration. This may not be the fault of the incentive program, but may be a problem of failing to provide proper information technology (IT) administrative support to the program.

Sales compensation *is* noisy. Sometimes the design is at fault, and sometimes it's an issue of alignment. It can even be just a by-product of an effective program. As a sales compensation designer, this book will help you sort out what problems are real and what are not, where the solution resides, and how to make the right changes.

JOB CONTENT—THE SOURCE OF SALES COMPENSATION DESIGN

When asked about the origin of a sales compensation program within a company, the response might include the following: "It's always been that way" or "It's the industry practice. We follow what others do."

These reasons may sound compelling, but they do not provide a strong rationale for designing effective sales compensation programs. Historical practices, sometimes known as legacy solutions, are often no longer contemporary with market realities or support a sales model that no longer exists.

What about industry practice? Follow industry practice only if your company is identical to your competitors and if they have found the ideal sales compensation solution. However, the likelihood that your products, customers, and customer coverage strategy are identical to your competitors is, at best, remote. So, following what others do in your industry is usually not an effective strategy. As we will learn later, the design of the sales compensation plan is unique to every company.

Effective sales compensation begins with the proper strategy alignment and ends with effective job design. There are several points where sales management *must* achieve alignment before reaching the sales compensation program. The right products must be aligned with the right customers. The right sales jobs must be aligned with the right buyers. The sales jobs must have clarity of purpose—alignment to the sales task—and the performance measures must have alignment with the job content.

Once sales management provides proper alignment among customers, products, and sales jobs, then sales management can craft a sales compensation plan to support the *aligned* sales strategy. As we will learn in Chapter 4, sales compensation design is driven by job content. Get the job right and the sales compensation design is easy. Conversely, create a confusing, misaligned sales job and no sales compensation plan can be successful.

SALES JOBS AND SALES PROCESS

The art and science of crafting effective sales compensation programs rest with a commanding competency in sales job design—assessment, evaluation, and construction. Job design errors are the No. 1 culprit in sales compensation plan failure.

Sales management configures sales jobs to serve a preferred target buyer population. All sales processes comprise five key components. Depending on the products, market, and customers, sales management will define the sales job within the context of these five components:

- *Demand creation:* Stimulating the market.
- *Buyer identification:* Finding the decision makers.
- *Purchase commitment:* Securing the order.
- *Order fulfillment:* Delivering the product or solution.
- *Customer support:* Providing ongoing support after the initial purchase.

Each step of the selling process contributes to securing and keeping customers. The sales job is often involved in each step of the sales process; however, the level of involvement varies significantly from one company to another and from one sales job to another. The following are descriptions of how sales personnel may be involved in each step.

- *Component 1: Demand Creation:* Typically, the marketing department has responsibility for demand creation. Through advertising, public relations, trade shows, and direct promotion, the marketing department creates demand for the company's products or services. However, in many cases, the sales department will help create demand for the product. This is usually true for companies selling new high-end products in the business-to-business market. This is known as "new market" selling. In these instances, the most practical method to create demand for the product is to hire a seasoned sales force to promote the product to target buyers. In some instances, some sales organizations, such as pharmaceutical sales, only do the first two steps of the sales process—demand creation and buyer identification—with no other sales process responsibility. In these instances, sales personnel promote products but never actually write the order.

- *Component 2: Buyer Identification:* It is normally the responsibility of sales personnel to identify buyers who can make a purchase decision. When selling complex products and services, identifying the buyer(s) can be extremely challenging. Many sales training programs and sales improvement programs spend considerable time educating sales personnel on how to work with the customers' numerous individuals and teams to correctly identify the right decision makers. However, in other companies, marketing, not sales personnel, assumes responsibility for both demand creation *and* buyer identification by having customers identify themselves through direct response either by mail, telephone, or Web site visits. Finally, in other companies, the marketing department is responsible for identifying potential buyers through research conducted by telemarketing reps. Marketing then assigns these potential buyers (hot leads) to the sales force for sales efforts.

- *Component 3: Purchase Commitment:* The primary value of a sales representative is to secure a purchase commitment from a customer. This step is typically known as "closing" the sale. We all share a common image of a sales rep opening up the order book and writing down the customer's order. (This is how the now seemingly quaint expression "book the order" came into the sales world vernacular.) While a high-tech version of booking the order still exists today, securing a purchase commitment can be an involved and complex process of contracts, fulfillment obligations, performance-pricing, and delivery commitments. For most companies, a booked order now arrives via an electronic medium. Still, some sales departments require their sales personnel to remain involved in every part of the transaction, ensuring that all elements of the purchase process have been successfully completed. At the other end of the spectrum, we find customers so well acquainted with products that they do not need or want a salesperson involved in the purchase process. These customers prefer to order by telephone, fax, or from an e-commerce Web site.

- *Component 4: Order Fulfillment:* The actual delivery of a product or service to a customer is collectively called "order fulfillment."

In some cases, the salesperson provides order fulfillment, but frequently this responsibility rests with others. But there are many selling models where sales organizations require sales personnel to oversee the successful delivery of the product to the customer. Customers will typically call the salesperson to check on the status of the order as they await delivery or ask for assistance if there is an order fulfillment problem.

- *Component 5: Customer Service:* Most sales organizations work collaboratively with customer service departments to provide after-the-sale support. Even so, sales representatives will occasionally find themselves involved in customer service issues if a customer is not satisfied with a product or service. In some companies, this is a mandated part of the sales job, and sales personnel will work with internal resources to ensure customer satisfaction.

Each of these activities—demand creation, buyer identification, purchase commitment, order fulfillment, and customer service—contribute to a successful sales process. The role of the salesperson will vary depending on products, customers, and the company's sales coverage model. The mix and configuration of these sales process roles determine the content of the sales job, and sales job content drives sales compensation design.

SALES COMPENSATION—PAYING FOR THE POINT OF PERSUASION

The highest value provided by sales personnel is to help customers make choices when there is uncertainty and risk. This event is known as the "point of persuasion." The purpose of sales compensation is to reward seller success at the point of persuasion.

While salesperson involvement in the sales process will vary from one sales job to another, the task of building the right sales compensation plan is greatly simplified by looking for the point of persuasion.

In most cases, we will find that the point of persuasion is at the *Purchase Commitment* sales process step, but not always. For example, the point of persuasion might be in the first step, *Demand Creation*, where the salesperson's point of persuasion is to cause the customer to learn more about a company's products. Conversely, it might be at a later stage in the sales process, such as at *Order Fulfillment*, when a customer is having second thoughts about the purchase and the salesperson must reassure the customer of the wisdom of the purchase. *Finding, defining, and measuring the point of persuasion is the focus of effective sales compensation design.*

SALES FORCE OBSOLESCENCE AND SALES COMPENSATION

Maintaining alignment and avoiding obsolescence is the continuing struggle of sales leadership. Sales force obsolescence is a natural occurrence for all sales departments. Over a period of time, most sales forces will become obsolete. By this, we do not mean that *salespeople* will become obsolete. It is the sales department (its strategy and its deployment model) that becomes obsolete. The outcome of accumulated misalignment among products, customers, and sales resources produces an obsolete sales force.

With this obsolescence, the point of persuasion can change, shift, or be diminished. To illustrate this point, consider the following question: "Would you buy a commercial poster/print of birds over the Internet?" Most people would answer this question, "Yes." The reason they would buy a print over the Internet is because they understand what a print is and its value. They certainly don't need the assistance of a salesperson. However, when the question is modified, people are not so sure they would buy a print over the Internet without the aid of a salesperson. For example, consider this restated question: "As your first investment in rare prints of birds, would you purchase a John James Audubon print from the Havell Edition of *Birds of America* over the Internet? Many people would answer, "No." Why would they answer, "No"? In one case, a person is willing to buy a print over the Internet; yet in another case the same person is not willing. The answer is simple. There is risk and uncertainty in purchasing a rare print. Until you have the personal expertise to reduce your risk and uncertainty, you will seek the assistance of an adviser such as an informed and respected salesperson.

Here is another example: "Would you buy a personal computer over the phone or via an e-commerce Web site?" Today, many longtime PC users purchase their computers without the assistance of a salesperson. However, when these same individuals were making their first PC purchase, they sought the advice and assurance of salespeople before they made their purchase decision.

So salespeople are ideally suited to be at the point where customers have risk and uncertainty—at the point of persuasion. As illustrated above, this point of persuasion is constantly on the move. Sales organizations and sales jobs can become obsolete as the point of persuasion moves beyond the current deployment model.

A dated coverage model nearly dooms an encyclopedia company. An encyclopedia company was late to realize that its sales coverage model was going to doom the company. The selling of encyclopedias has a long and proud history of providing personal in-home sales contact to parents looking to acquire additional educational support for their children. Expensive, with annual updates and custom furniture, a multivolume encyclopedia was traditionally a significant purchase. The company's authorized in-home sales agents sold within exclusive territories. The company provided no other channel to buy the product. The company was loyal to its agents—to a fault. As parents became more sophisticated, the rise of mega bookstores offering multivolume encyclopedias occurred. New competitors entered the market including CD encyclopedias and free Web-based encyclopedias and the in-house sales agents became a sales coverage liability. Long past the point of obvious need for change, the company abandoned its use of a single sales channel, almost too late.

Preferred Solution: Monitor sales coverage models actively. Preclude sales channel obsolescence by moving quickly to keep sales personnel aligned with buyer populations.

THE IMPACT OF CUSTOMER RELATIONSHIP MANAGEMENT

The promise of customer relationship management (CRM) is to provide a single-technology platform for tracking and managing the sales process. With a common technology platform, CRM offers the opportunity for assigning and managing elements of the sales process continuum to divergent parties while successfully keeping track of all customer interactions. In this respect, CRM can alter sales job content. As a company shifts parts of the sales process to other resources, what role does the salesperson perform? Remember, the definition of this revised job role is the starting point for effective sales compensation design.

SUMMARY

Sales compensation works as part of a complex management process. Look to job content as the source for designing effective sales compensation plans. Locate the point of persuasion and reward the salesperson for making a difference—that is where sales compensation belongs.

Chapter 2

Sales Compensation Fundamentals

In this chapter, we will review key sales compensation fundamentals. First, we will review variable compensation models and then examine why sales compensation is unique. Next, we will discuss the difference between income producers and sales representatives. Lastly, we will examine sales compensation design elements.

VARIABLE COMPENSATION MODELS

Figure 2-1 depicts five different types of common variable compensation models.

The chart divides all incentive plans into two major categories: "Target Rate" and "Target Pay." A "unit rate" plan has a fixed commission schedule or piece rate that pays for each increment of performance—another sales dollar, another garment sewn. Target pay plans begin with a target labor market pay level for the job obtained by compensation planners using benchmark surveys. Management will either adjust this market number up or down to reflect the company's pay strategy. For example, real estate agents have a "commission rate" plan. Management does not manage pay with the use of quotas and formulas to reach or exceed a target

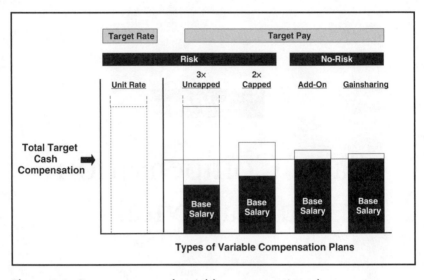

Figure 2-1 Common types of variable compensation plans.

pay amount. Instead, the real estate sales persons know their commission rate—a well-established number in the market—and they produce unit sales to achieve sales results.

A second division featured in Figure 2-1 groups the incentive plans into "No-Risk" and "Risk" plans. A "no-risk" plan has no reduction in the target total cash compensation reducing the base salary below this target amount. Instead, the incentive plan provides additional monies—over-target pay—for over-target performance. "At-Risk" plans pay a reduced base salary, as a portion of the target total cash compensation. Incumbents earn additional monies for reaching minimum, at-target, and exceeding-target performance levels.

The horizontal line reflects the target total cash compensation (TTCC) for the job. We depict the base salary amount as dark shading while variable dollars have no shading. Notice that the first plan type has no base salary. These are Unit Rate plans where the employee receives a payment for each unit of accomplishment such as a commission on sales dollars. The next two plans—3× Uncapped and 2× Capped—have pay at-risk. The base pay is less than the total target cash compensation. The last two plans—Add-On and Gainsharing—have a full base salary with no variable pay below TTCC.

The characteristics and application of these five common pay systems differ from one another.

- *Unit Rate:* A Unit Rate plan pays a fixed amount (dollars or percent of dollars) for each unit of performance. Income producers such as traders, real estate agents, and mortgage origination professionals earn payouts under producer plans. The same logic of payment per unit applies to piece rate workers, too.

   Sellers who are income producers create business revenue. Their value is not in the products they offer, but the relationships they manage. In many cases, they sell commodities. What is unique is their relationship with their customers; they often have the power to take their customers with them when they change employers. Typically, income producers have no base salary and earn a fixed commission on all sales. Although management may identify a preferred earnings level, the commission rate is a more important consideration for income producers. Income producers evaluate the competitiveness of pay by the size of the commission rate.

- *3× Uncapped Plans:* 3× Uncapped plans provide an upside earning opportunity that is 3 times the at-risk component without a cap on earnings. This 3× upside is provided to those who reach the 90th percentile of performance among peer performers. Ten percent of this group may actually exceed this number making the plan still "managed," but "uncapped." This is the most common design for sales professionals.

   A sales representative *represents* the value of his or her company's products, services, and solutions. The inherent value of the relationship between the company and its customer rests with the company's value proposition. It is the role of the sales representative to present this value proposition to all customers to affect sales. The ratio between base salary and target incentive pay as a portion of TTCC varies by job content. The more the salesperson can influence a customer to act, the lower the base salary as a portion of target total cash compensation and the higher the at-risk component. The opposite is also true: The less personal influence inherent in a sales job to affect customer buying decisions, the higher the base salary and the lower the incentive opportunity. Upside earning opportunities are set at 3 times the at-risk component; thus the payout level for outstanding performance is known as a "triple." Performance measures are tied to sales production. Payouts begin for below-target performance and may or may not have a performance threshold. A preferred performance distribution features two-thirds reaching and exceeding quota and one-third not reaching quota. Sales management helps achieve this performance distribution through effective quota setting. These plans avoid pay caps. Ten percent or fewer of individuals will exceed the triple upside earnings level. Management accomplishes this upside earnings control through sound formula construction and effective quota assignment. When communicating to participants, sales management presents the target total compensation, the base pay, and the formula to earn and exceed target compensation.

- *2× Capped Plans:* Stated as a percentage of base salary, a 2× Capped plan percent bonus targets vary from as low as 10 percent of base salary to as high as 100 percent of base salary, depending on the job level. Most management incentive plans (MIPs) use 2× Capped plans. Target bonus and target base salary combine to equal total target cash compensation with payouts tied to a combination of corporate, business unit, and individual performance results. Participants can earn payouts for below-target performance. 2× Capped plans provide twice the target earnings as an upside opportunity for outstanding performance. Most management bonus plans have a high performance threshold and usually don't have any restriction on the number of participants who receive a payout, but most plans cap the upside at 2 times the target incentive percent. Sales support jobs and consumer package goods sellers often participate in a 2× Capped plan.

- *Add-on Plans:* Management uses add-on pay plans in a variety of circumstances. While gainsharing plans tend to be all-inclusive, add-on plans target specific work units, jobs, or people. Add-on plans provide a target dollar earning or a target percentage of base salary for accomplishment of pre-established goals. Some add-on plans are permanent and ongoing, for example, "10 percent of base salary paid to the most productive top 10 percent of customer service representatives." Other add-on plans serve short-term purposes such as contests and special program incentive funds (SPIFs). They fit numerous situations and provide additional pay for individual or unit performance. Payouts occur only for above-goal performance and average 5 to 10 percent of base salaries. While normally very effective, add-on plans have downside risks. Too many duplicate plans, excessive payments, inappropriate goals, and inconsistent eligibility criteria can weaken add-on plans.

- *Gainsharing:* Corporate gainsharing plans help drive overall corporate success by tying payouts to corporate results. Gainsharing plans have no pay at risk and therefore present no downside cost to the employee. Most corporate gainsharing plans tie payouts to a percentage of corporate revenue or profit. In this manner, management shares the incremental gain with employees on a prespecified proportional basis. Sometimes local management will use a gainsharing plan to help boost productivity. Generally, all employees participate in the gainsharing plan with no restriction on the number of employees who can receive a payout.

Normally, participants earn no payout unless the company or unit reaches its stated goal. Gainsharing plans target between 3 and 8 percent of base salary for payout purposes, although this number varies by company and wage inflation trends. These programs tend to surge in popularity every 10 to 15 years. Gainsharing plans have a mixed history of success. The most successful programs succeed as a result of high-level commitment by corporate leadership. Unfortunately, gainsharing plans fail when participants view the program as an entitlement. An entitlement perspective produces the following results: Payouts in good years garner only modest satisfaction, while no payouts in bad years produce significant dissatisfaction.

INCOME PRODUCERS VERSUS SALES REPRESENTATIVES

It is easy to confuse the income producers with sales representatives and vice versa. Income producers and sales representatives are very much alike. They sell products to customers. They both earn incentive compensation for sales results. They even share similar commission formula types. However, the underlying economic principles differ between income producers and sales representatives. Income producers split a portion of their commission—sales transaction earnings—with their employer. For example, stockbrokers earn a commission on every buy or sell transaction. Part of the commission is paid to the stockbroker—the income producer—and part to the brokerage house. Often, income producers receive no base salary or a modest draw. Sales revenue provides the funding for income producer payments. Competitiveness of pay is evaluated by comparing commission rates, and actual compensation levels are less relevant. In fact, employers encourage high earnings as additional dollars are shared between the employer and the income producer. The more the income producer makes, the more the company makes. Scant attention is given to high or low payments.

Over the long run, macro labor market trends make adjustments to income producers' earnings by increasing or decreasing the number of income producers working in the market, and, as a result, employment levels closely mimic the expansion and contraction of income-producer markets.

On the other hand, the underlying economic model for sales representatives differs from income producers. Sales management identifies a Total Target Cash Compensation and performance expectations for the sales representative job. Sales management calibrates incentive formula and quota levels to ensure that payouts conform to expected performance distribution for minimal, target, and outstanding pay expectations.

Whereas the income producer's pay level is managed by sales production multiplied by the commission rate, the sales representative's pay is always managed as compared to a preferred target compensation level. As a sales representative performs against target performance, a portion of the incentive compensation is awarded—low performance earns low pay, and high performance earns high pay; all are measured in relation to the target incentive amount.

The relationship of pay and sales volume is usually linear for income producers. As Figure 2-2 illustrates, the more products sold, the higher the payout.

Figure 2-2 Relationship between earnings and sales volume for income producers.

Figure 2-3 Relationship between earnings and sales volume for sales representatives.

However, the relationship between earnings and volume is not linear for sales representatives as shown in Figure 2-3. Earnings increase as sales volume increases, but at a decreasing rate.

When compared to Figure 2-4, the pay lines for income producers and sales representatives clearly differ.

Labor market practices continue to provide higher pay levels to sales representatives, but at a decreasing rate as compared to sales production volume. The job level structure embeds this declining proportional value of target pay versus the production volume. Figure 2-5 demonstrates that target pay continues to increase in each job, but at a decreasing rate.

We will examine more income producer pay issues later in the book. Let's now return to sales representative issues.

Figure 2-4 Comparison of earnings versus volume for income producers and sales reps.

Figure 2-5 Decreasing rate of pay increases at various job levels.

ABOUT SALES COMPENSATION CONCEPTS

In this next section, you will find highlighted boxes featuring sales compensation concepts. Each concept states a best-practice solution.

> **Key Concept:** *Sales Representatives Self-Fund Their Sales Compensation Payments.* While sales revenue funds sales compensation payments for income producers, sales representatives fund their own sales compensation program. This occurs as the sales compensation program redistributes the at-risk monies. Better performers make more than their target at-risk incentive pay, and poor performers make less than their at-risk target incentive pay. While the math does not always fit perfectly—sometimes more is paid, sometimes less is paid—the concept is clear: Sales representatives collectively fund their sales compensation plan through redistribution of the target at-risk incentive compensation dollars.

The remaining material in this chapter addresses design elements for sales representatives. We will revisit sales compensation design choices in Chapter 5, "Formula Types."

SALES COMPENSATION DESIGN ELEMENTS FOR SALES REPRESENTATIVES

Sales compensation design elements are the building blocks of effective sales compensation plans. Each sales compensation plan is the summation of decisions made about these design elements. The design elements are as follows:

- Eligibility
- Target total cash compensation
- Pay mix and leverage
- Performance measures and weights
- Quota distribution
- Performance range
- Performance and payment periods

Decisions about these design elements must be made before selecting the appropriate formula.

All sales compensation plans for sales representative jobs share these same design elements. A company can build a coherent overall sales compensation program by adopting one set of design principles for all design elements. Sales management can then apply these design principles to all sales jobs when building job-specific sales compensation plans. In this manner, sales management creates a sales compensation program consisting of individual sales compensation plans; yet each plan is consistent with the company's design principles.

Key Concept: *Sales Compensation Plans Should Equal the Number of Sales Jobs.* Sales compensation follows sales job design. Sales compensation supports the sales management objectives for each sales job. Sales compensation plans are not designed for individual salespeople unless the individual is a single incumbent for a job. The number of unique sales compensation plans should be equal to the number of unique sales jobs.

ELIGIBILITY

Which jobs should be eligible for sales compensation? There are many different types of jobs within the sales department. Not all of them should be eligible for sales compensation plan participation.

Establishing a job eligibility policy will resolve confusion regarding which jobs and their incumbents should participate in the sales compensation program. This decision about sales compensation plan eligibility does not preclude noneligible jobs and their incumbents from participating in other incentive plans such as gainsharing, add-on plans, and management bonus plans. The most common eligibility criteria require job incumbents to (1) have customer contact and (2) persuade the customer to act in a positive financial benefit to the company. Of course, this would include salespeople, telesales, channel sales representatives, and many other customer contact personnel. It would usually exclude such jobs as the district manager's secretary or headquarters product managers.

However, companies do adopt different practices than the one stated above. Some companies are more expansive with their eligibility rules and other companies are more restrictive. Regardless, a company needs to establish the criteria for sales compensation eligibility. Absent such a policy, ongoing confusion about which jobs are or are not eligible for sales compensation will arise.

Sample Eligibility Policy: For a job to be eligible to participate in the sales compensation program, the incumbents must (1) have customer contact and (2) persuade the customer to act in a positive financial benefit to the company.

Your Eligibility Policy:

TARGET TOTAL CASH COMPENSATION

Sales personnel who reach expected performance earn Target Total Cash Compensation (TTCC). Depending on individual performance, some sales representatives will earn more and some will earn less.

Using survey data and applying management judgment, management establishes a TTCC for each job.

The total remuneration for sales jobs includes the following cash and noncash components:

- *Base salary:* Most sales representatives receive a base salary.
- *Sales compensation:* Sales compensation is the variable pay tied to sales performance.
- *Benefits:* Sales representatives participate in the company's benefit programs.
- *Contests/SPIFs:* Management uses add-on contests and SPIFs, or special program incentive funds, to reward special efforts.
- *Recognition events:* Most companies provide a special annual recognition event for outstanding salespeople.
- *Expense reimbursement:* Expense reimbursement pays out-of-pocket costs of sales representatives.

Target total cash compensation includes both the base salary and the sales compensation components. It excludes benefits, contests and/or SPIFs, recognition events, and sales expense reimbursement.

Key Concept: *Don't Overpay or Underpay for Sales Performance.* For sales representatives, don't significantly overpay or underpay for sales performance as compared to market practices. High pay will incur excessive sales costs, while underpayment will escalate costs in other areas such as low productivity, high turnover, and poor morale. Ensure market comparisons are consistent with the range of sales performance by matching expected payouts to the survey data for the 25th, 50th, and 75th percentile of market payout amounts.

Setting the correct TTCC requires collecting accurate external pay data and making judgments regarding internal equity among all the sales jobs, and perhaps other jobs within the company.

Some companies prefer to take a more aggressive competitive pay position as compared to labor market rates, while others prefer to be more conservative. Regardless, sales management needs to review and manage TTCC consistently from year to year. This includes capturing external labor market data from reliable survey sources on an annual basis and making necessary adjustments to target pay levels.

Sample Target Total Cash Compensation Policy: Set the TTCC for each job at the 60th percentile of market practices as presented in the annual industry survey. Payouts for poor performers will be equal to the 25th percentile of pay; top performers will earn payouts equal to or greater than the 90th percentile of labor market rates.

Your Target Total Cash Compensation Policy:

_____

_____

PAY MIX AND LEVERAGE

Pay mix and leverage together provide the range of pay opportunities based on sales performance.

- *Pay mix:* Pay mix splits TTCC into two components: base salary and target incentive amount. We express pay mix as a percentage split with the first number representing the base salary and the second number representing target incentive amount:

Base Salary/Target Incentive

These two percentage amounts added together always equal 100 percent.

Examples:	**90/10**	Base Salary = 90% of TTCC
		Target Incentive = 10% of TTCC
	75/25	Base Salary = 75% of TTCC
		Target Incentive = 25% of TTCC

For a TTCC of $100,000, the 90/10 pay mix provides a target base salary of $90,000 and a target incentive opportunity of $10,000. A pay mix of 75/25 for the same TTCC of $100,000 provides a target base salary of $75,000 and a target incentive opportunity of $25,000.

Pay mix varies by job content. Generally, as the relative influence of the sales representative increases, the lower the base salary component and the higher the target incentive amount. For example, a new account territory sales job might have a pay mix of 60/40 whereas a major account sales job might have a pay mix of 80/20. The average pay mix for business-to-business territory sales representatives in the United States is approximately 70/30. However, there is a wide variance to this national norm.

Figure 2-6 shows different levels of pay mix with 100/0 having no pay at risk and 0/100 with 100 percent of the TTCC at risk.

- *Leverage:* Leverage is a mathematical expression for the upside earning potential for a sales job. We express leverage as a multiplier of the target incentive. The most common leverage is known as a "triple." For notation purposes, it is normally written as "3×." Do not confuse leverage as a pay cap. The leverage amount provides an upside earnings estimate for the best performers. For definition purposes, we define *best performers* as the 90th percentile of performance among all job incumbents. In other words, the best performers receive three times the target

Figure 2-6 Various levels of pay mix.

incentive for outstanding sales performance, defined as the 90th percentile of sales personnel for that job.

The triple rule of leverage (3×) is a shorthand method to replicate what takes place in the labor market. However, certain companies will intentionally pay more than a triple leverage, such as 3.5× or 4×, to provide more aggressive pay for their top performers. Or they will pay less than a triple leverage, say 2.5×, for their top performers, presuming the labor market does not support 3× for the best performers. The company does not need to pay market pay levels. As with any target pay level, management judgment is the ultimate source for setting upside incentive opportunity. However, labor market practices for 75th and 90th percentile of the labor market pay levels provide an excellent reference point for evaluating a proposed leverage.

Pay mix and leverage provide the range of pay opportunities available to sales personnel.

Figure 2-7 shows the complete relationship among the following components: target total cash compensation, base salary, target incentive, upside incentive, pay mix, and leverage.

Sample Pay Mix and Leverage Policy: Each job has its own pay mix depending on degree of personal influence configured into the job design. Territory sales jobs will have a pay mix of 70/30 and major

Pay Mix and Leverage

Figure 2-7 Relationship among compensation components.

account sales jobs will have a pay mix of 80/20. The leverage for individual contributor sales territory jobs will be 3×; overlay specialists 2.75×; and first-line sales supervisors 2.5×. The leverage for new market sellers is 3.5×.

Your Pay Mix and Leverage Policy:

PERFORMANCE MEASURES AND WEIGHTS

The art of designing effective sales compensation formulas rests with the discipline of selecting and weighting the right performance measures. The selection of the performance measures for inclusion in the sales compensation plan marks the point where strategy translates into tactics. When sales management selects a performance measure for the sales compensation program, then sales leadership officially sanctions that measure.

Once the leadership team selects the performance measures, the next step is to establish the relative importance of each measure. This is done by *weighting* the performance measures. Below, we examine concepts related to selecting and weighting of performance measures.

Selecting Performance Measures

The uniqueness of any sales compensation rests with its performance measures. There are dozens of different types of performance measures, but the most common and most practical fall into five major categories:

- *Volume production measures:* Volume production measures are the most popular and appropriate performance measures for sales compensation purposes. Production measures include three categories: sales revenue (purchase, continuing, renewed, and estimated), profit dollars (gross margin, contribution margin), and items (units, contracts, and design-wins).

- *Sales effectiveness measures:* Sales effectiveness measures help improve sales results by focusing sales efforts in the areas of product (balance, mix, launch, cross-sell, packages, solutions), accounts (new, retained, penetrate, growth, win-back), orders (close rate, size, length of contract, linearity, and receivables), and price management (discounts, rebates, realization, and percent change).

- *Customer impact measures:* Customer impact measures evaluate sales satisfaction (customer surveys, number of complaints) and loyalty (order persistency, market share, and comparative loyalty survey scores).

- *Resource utilization measures:* Resource utilization measures confirm the effective use of resources including the following measures: productivity (cost per order dollar, quota sales loading), channels (partner success, partner participation rates, outlet performance), and subordinates (for supervisors—balance performance, turnover, and new hire ramp rate).

- *Weighting performance measures:* Senior management confirms the importance of each performance measure by allocating a portion of 100 percent to each of the measures.

Key Concept: *Use No More Than Three Output Measures in a Sales Compensation Plan.* Sales compensation plans work best with three or fewer performance measures. Limiting performance measures ensures that those selected get the full attention of the sales force. Use output measures tied to actual sales results and avoid input measures such as presales activity measures, for example, number of sales calls or proposals written.

Performance Measures

	Sales Volume	Product Mix	Retention
Weighting:	55%	25%	20%

No single measure should be worth less than 15 percent. The summation of the weights always equals 100 percent. Each job has its own unique set of performance measures and weights.

Sample Performance Selection and Weighting Policy: A sales compensation plan will have three or fewer output performance measures. No measure will be worth less than 15 percent of the total weighting. The primary measure of sales success is net sales revenue performance less service contract revenue. All plans will have a customer loyalty measure representing 15 percent of the value of the incentive plan.

Your Performance Selection and Weighting Policy:

_____

_____

QUOTA DISTRIBUTION

Quota distribution establishes the desired difficulty of quotas. If quotas are too easy, the sales compensation plan might overpay. If quotas are too difficult, the sales compensation program could underpay. A preferred quota distribution target is to have two-thirds of the salespeople reaching and exceeding quota and one-third not. This distribution of performance allows for the cross-funding of upside pay to high performers by shifting a share of the low performer's target incentive pay to the better performers.

This distribution of two-thirds over quota and one-third below quota is a target distribution outcome. In some years, the distribution may be skewed in one direction or the other. However, over

Figure 2-8 The two-thirds/one-third quota distribution split.

the long run, the distribution should favor the split of two-thirds exceeding quota and one-third not exceeding quota.

Figure 2-8 shows this preferred two-thirds reaching and exceeding quota and one-third not reaching quota.

A more mathematically rigorous model might suggest a target of 50/50 quota distribution, with 50 percent exceeding quota and 50 percent not reaching quota to ensure that the cross-funding of below-quota performers and above-quota performers is in balance. However, due to the use of thresholds and the impact of terminations, the two-thirds versus one-third model seems to provide the right cross-funding balance.

Record-breaking unit sales, bad quota performance. The sales force for a contact lens company had broken all unit sales records. However, the VP of Sales had to contend with a morale problem because only 5 percent of the sales personnel reached sales revenue quota. Even though the company was being lauded for its sales prowess, fewer than 5 percent of sales personnel would earn target incentive pay. A price war on contact lenses ignited dramatic sales growth. Because quotas were established and measured in revenue, sales success—defined as revenue performance—dropped as the company took substantial market share by using a low price strategy. They sold a lot more lenses at lower prices, but still did not hit their revenue goals. High unit sales success could not offset the lower price per unit. Sales personnel could not reach their sales revenue goals.

Preferred Solution: The price collapse negated the basic premise of the quotas. In this case, sales management needed to terminate the old plan and redesign a new plan with new quotas to match the company's emerging market dynamics.

Sample Quota Distribution Policy: The summation of all quota assignments should equal the company budget forecast. Quota distribution targets two-thirds of all sales personnel for a job to reach and exceed quota, and one-third not to reach quota.

Your Quota Distribution Policy:

PERFORMANCE RANGE

Performance range specifies the low and high spread of performance for payment purposes. The low point of this range represents minimal performance where performance below this level should *not* receive incentive payment. The high point of this range represents excellent performance where outstanding performance should receive outstanding pay, such as 3× leverage. The performance range of a measure differs from one measure to another, from one job to another, from one company to another, and from one industry to another. As an example, the performance range for an established consumer product is normally very narrow. Salespeople will find it unlikely to sell above 105 percent of goal. Likewise, the chance of falling below 95 percent of goal is also remote. Mature consumer products have a very predictable and narrow performance range. On the other hand, new growth industries might have a very wide

Figure 2-9 Sample threshold performance range—from 70 to 145 percent.

performance range. As an example, sales of 200 percent over goal might be the norm for exceptional performance while 50 percent of goal might be considered typical minimal performance. Each performance measure has its own performance range. Sales management can best determine the performance range for a given measure by examining its historical range.

In Figure 2-9, the performance range is from 70 to 145 percent. Low performers (10th percentile) perform at or below 70 percent to quota. Excellent performers achieve 145 percent of quota where the top 10th percentile will perform and should receive outstanding pay.

In Figure 2-10, the performance range is 80 percent for low performers and 120 percent for excellent performers.

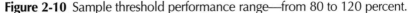

Figure 2-10 Sample threshold performance range—from 80 to 120 percent.

Sales management needs to identify the performance range for each measure in each sales compensation plan. As we learn later, we will use this information to build the sales compensation formula rates.

Sample Performance Range Policy: Threshold and excellence performance levels will be set for each performance measure. Threshold reflects the lower 10 percent of performance, and excellence represents the top 10 percent of performance.

Your Performance Range Policy:

_____

_____

PERFORMANCE AND PAYMENT PERIODS

Performance periods and payment periods work together. Sales management sets the performance period for each formula measure—the length of time between performance measurement periods. This window of time can be a week, month, quarter, or even as long as a year. Shorter sales cycles generally have shorter performance periods; longer sales cycles generally have longer performance periods. The payment period determines when the incentive payment occurs. Normally, the performance period and the payment period are the same, for example, measured and paid quarterly. Additionally, performance and/or payment periods can be discrete or cumulative.

* *Discrete:* Discrete performance/payment periods stand alone for measurement and payment purpose. For example, a sales compensation plan that pays "monthly discrete" treats each month as a stand-alone measurement and payment period. No previous or future month's performance will affect the payout for an

individual month. Use less than annual discrete measurement periods when sales cycles are short and sales personnel have no flexibility or self-serving motivation to move orders from one period to another.

- *Cumulative:* Use a cumulative performance/payment period when you want the salesperson to be paid at more frequent intervals than the ultimate measurement period. As an example, "paid quarterly on cumulative year-to-date performance" provides payouts each quarter based on year-to-date performance.

Figure 2-11 displays both discrete and cumulative performance measurement and payment periods.

As the cumulative period to date, Performance/Payment periods demonstrate in Figure 2-11, the salesperson always carries the responsibility for year-to-date performance even though payouts are being made on a quarterly basis. Each quarter, the year-to-date

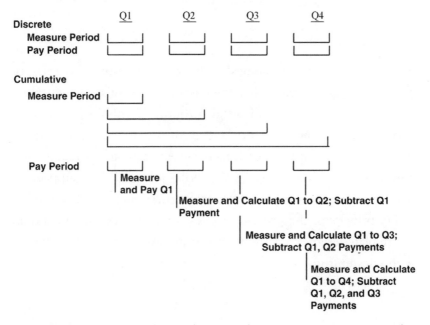

Figure 2-11 Discrete and cumulative performance measurement and payment periods.

performance and incentive are calculated. To make the quarterly payments, any previous quarterly payments are subtracted from this year-to-date amount before the final payment for the quarter is made.

A sales compensation plan might have several formula components. Some might be paid with a discrete performance/payment period while others might be paid with cumulative period-to-date performance/payment period.

Sample Performance/Payment Period Policy: Sales personnel are responsible for year-to-date sales performance. More frequent payouts can be made on a cumulative year-to-date basis.

Your Performance/Payment Period Policy:

_____

_____

SUMMARY

A company needs to establish sales compensation principles of eligibility, target total cash compensation, pay mix and leverage, performance measures and weights, quota distribution, performance range, and performance and payment periods to effectively manage sales compensation practices. As markets, products, and corporate objectives change, so will sales jobs and their supporting sales compensation plans. By documenting the company's overriding principles, the process of sales compensation design should create plan designs consistent with corporate principles, but aligned with sales unit goals.

Chapter 3

Who Owns Sales Compensation?

"Who owns the sales compensation program?" might seem like an academic question to some. "The sales department" is the obvious answer; yet when we examine this issue more closely, we find many players are involved in the design and management of the sales compensation program. Sales wants to drive performance. Marketing and product management wants focus on select products. Finance wants a fiscally responsible pay program. The human resources department wants total target cash compensation (TTCC) to be externally competitive and internally equitable with nonsales jobs. The information technology (IT) department wants to provide timely and accurate administrative support and legal wants legally protected and compliant pay programs. Not surprisingly, the CEO of the company wants the sales compensation program to support the strategy of each business unit.

A recent edition of the annual *Sales Compensation Trends Survey*, as published by The Alexander Group, found that among 270 medium to large companies, the final approval for sales compensation plan designs rests almost 50 percent of the time with the CEO, COO, or General Manager.

48.48%	CEO, COO, or General Manager
28.41%	Sales Management/Sales Operations
9.47%	Senior Executive Compensation Committee
4.55%	Sales Compensation Design Task Force
4.17%	HR/Compensation
1.52%	Board of Directors
1.52%	Other
1.14%	Finance
0.76%	Marketing

While the survey responses support the sales management as the ultimate authority, note the involvement of the chief executive officer (CEO)/general manager. Even after eliminating the statistical impact of small sales forces from the survey data, the CEO/general manager is still the ultimate authority for the sales compensation plan for 25 percent of the reporting sales organizations having more than 100 sales representatives.

The sales compensation program (base salary and incentive payments) helps drive revenue growth but also represents a significant financial cost to the company. For a sales force of more than 100 eligible employees, the sales compensation program can have an annual budget between $10 and $20 million. The accountable revenues can be between $100 and $250 million—and the larger the sales force, the larger the costs and attendant revenue commitment. The point is sales compensation budgets are large, their revenue impact is significant, and they require active management—by multiple parties—to be successful.

SALES COMPENSATION PROGRAM OWNERSHIP

Although the sales compensation program must serve many (and often competing) objectives, it is still a sales management program. It is part of an array of management tools used by the sales department to manage sales productivity. It does not sit independent of a fully integrated sales management model. We suggest that the sales department act as the steward of the sales compensation program. But others, such as the CEO/general manager, marketing, finance, and human resources, must have access to the design, management, and administration of the sales compensation program.

In this chapter, we present sales compensation program accountabilities and suggest appropriate program responsibilities—who should do what to make sure the sales compensation program works effectively.

PROGRAM ACCOUNTABILITIES

The following program accountabilities support successful management of the sales compensation program:

- *Strategic alignment:* As corporate objectives migrate regarding markets, products, revenue growth, and profit goals, sales management must continually update the sales department to support these changing business objectives. Sometimes, major changes in strategy require major organizational changes creating new sales entities, new jobs, and new accountabilities. Other changes might be more subtle and can be made within the context of the existing sales organization. Whether the changes are major or minor, sales management, in most cases, must realign the sales compensation program to support new goals. Ongoing strategic realignment of the sales compensation program caused by changing corporate objectives confirms the need for periodic review and update of the sales compensation plans.
- *Effective design:* Sales compensation plans have numerous features and components. An effective design will properly support strategic objectives of the company and work correctly by

providing the right payouts for different levels of actual performance. Additionally, all sales compensation plans must work in concert with one another so that the overall sales compensation program (including crediting practices, quota allocation, and account assignments policies) works in logical unison. An effective sales compensation design ensures that all program features and components work together correctly.

- *Plan management:* Communication, training, interpretations, and adjustments are part of successful sales compensation program management. Plan rollout is the primary communication event for the sales compensation program. Communication also includes documentation, promotion, and feedback, and easy access via dedicated Web sites. New hires and newly appointed sales managers need training on the application of the sales compensation program. Plan provision interpretation occurs regularly due to unforeseen events, and minor design issues and adjustments will occasionally need to be made to fix problems.
- *Program administration:* Day-to-day administration of the program ensures proper sales crediting, payroll payment files, and management reporting.
- *Program assessment:* Regular assessment tests the sales compensation program for success. Numerous assessment methods examine strategic intent, competitiveness of pay, management utility, and sales force motivation.
- *Audit and legal review:* Finance audits and legal reviews keep the sales compensation program compliant with company guidelines and policies.

Whether you have a sales department of five sales representatives or a large sales department of 5,000 sales representatives, each of the above-mentioned program accountabilities exists in your organization. Someone has to do each of these tasks. For a small sales force, it might be the CEO or the vice president of sales doing them all. In larger sales organizations, these tasks are allocated to various parties as we describe in the next section.

ASSIGNMENT OF PROGRAM ACCOUNTABILITIES—LARGE SALES ORGANIZATIONS

The following presents possible accountability assignments by job role. While this is not a prescriptive model, it does provide an outline of traditional responsibilities for large sales departments. ("Large," in this case, means more than 200 sales personnel.)

- *CEO/Business unit general manager:* The CEO/business unit general manager must articulate the business objectives and goals to the sales department. The business unit general manager must also approve final plan designs to ensure alignment with business objectives and goals.
- *Vice president of sales:* The vice president (VP) of sales has overall responsibility for the sales compensation program. With the sales management leadership team, the VP of sales determines the proper role for sales compensation in the mix of the sales management model. Final accountability for sales compensation program effectiveness rests with the VP of sales.
- *VP of marketing:* The vice president of marketing provides information about product strategy and customer segments. The VP of marketing also needs to confirm that the sales compensation program correctly supports product marketing campaigns and promotions.
- *VP of finance:* The vice president of finance oversees the financial viability of the sales compensation program, ensuring that its costs and benefits are consistent with company objectives.
- *Sales operations:* Sales operations provide day-to-day management of the sales compensation program. This includes plan oversight, management, and reporting.

- *Field sales management:* Field sales management provides ongoing execution and evaluation of the sales compensation program. By providing the field perspective, field sales management helps assure program effectiveness and practicality.
- *Human resources:* The compensation manager provides external competitive market practices by purchasing reliable survey data. The compensation manager also examines internal equity of program fairness as compared to compensation programs provided to various nonsales jobs.
- *Legal:* The legal department approves plan documentation and program management to assure compliance with legal obligations.
- *Sales personnel:* Sales management solicits feedback from sales personnel through field interviews, focus group sessions, surveys, and one-on-one interviews with first-line sales managers.

The Costly Sales Force. The chief financial officer (CFO) became alarmed at the increasing relative cost of sales and called for a review of compensation levels. However, on review, the pay levels proved competitive with external pay levels. The market for test and measurement equipment is cyclical. The CFO noted that the company's cost of sales was increasing at a greater rate than competitors' cost of sales. Additional market analysis demonstrated that competitors' pay practices were more variable—less base salary and greater use of variable compensation. While not clear to the CFO, he presumed the compensation program was most likely contributing to the high cost of sales. When examined, the pay levels, regardless of pay mix, were very similar to those of sales personnel at the competitors. The CFO was correct on one account: The sales force was too costly. However, it was not the pay program. Further research showed that sales force productivity was lagging behind the competitors. While the quota sizes were comparative, the overall number of managerial, overlay specialists, marketing personnel, and headquarters staff was way above competitor levels.

Preferred Solution: Leave the sales head count and compensation plan alone; reduce staffing everywhere else.

USING COMMITTEES

We recommend the use of several sales compensation committees when feasible. To be effective, sales compensation plans frequently must reconcile competing objectives. A committee approach can best help raise and resolve these divergent issues. The following is an example of various types of sales compensation committees. Use them to drive best thinking, collaboration, and effectiveness of design.

- *Sales compensation design team:* We believe companies should entrust the design of the sales compensation program to a working committee represented by sales, field management, finance, marketing, and human resources. Charter this committee to examine current practices and suggest new sales compensation solutions for the next operating period.

SHOULD SALES REPRESENTATIVES SIT ON THE SALES COMPENSATION DESIGN TEAM?

Companies report success in having sales representatives as part of the sales compensation design team. As consultants, we try to avoid this practice. Yes, we want input from the field personnel about the current program, but the leadership team needs to make company-serving decisions about changes to the sales compensation program. Putting sales representatives on such a committee may compromise them with their peers or management and might misdirect the need to take new or dissimilar actions. Finally, participating in meetings about making pay changes may be protected activities as defined by the National Labor Relations Act so companies should check with their lawyers first before inviting a sales representative to sit on their design team.

- *Sales compensation leadership committee:* Many business units have a management committee comprised of sales, marketing, operations, and finance leaders. The leadership committee can specify the company's sales compensation design principles, reconfirm the business objectives, and approve plans as drafted by the sales compensation design team.

- *Sales compensation program management committee:* The program management committee has an ongoing responsibility for providing oversight to the sales compensation program application and interpretation. Meeting once a quarter, this committee can review and make decisions on program adjustments, plan exceptions, and policy interpretations. Additionally, this committee can provide ongoing program reviews by evaluating assessment reports prepared by sales operations and finance. It is a prudent exercise to completely document all decisions.

- *Sales compensation administration team:* For some organizations, program administration is significant, requiring continual oversight and management. In larger organizations, the administration of the sales compensation program might be shared by various parties such as sales operations, finance, commission accounting, payroll, and IT. Companies should bring these responsible parties together into a committee to make sure administration issues are resolved quickly, checks are issued in a timely manner, and real-time reports are available to management and sales personnel.

SALES COMPENSATION—THE PROCESS MANAGER

Appoint a process manager to oversee the whole sales compensation program including alignment, design, management, administration, assessment, audit, and legal. The process manager might report to sales and be found in the sales operations department. However, it's not uncommon for the process manager to come from another department. For example, this individual might be found in human resources, finance, or marketing. It's not important where the person sits; the most important thing is that he or she has the skills to manage all the complex issues related to sales compensation design. No one should presume that this position is the sales compensation czar. Instead, the appointed person should manage the process of sales compensation program design, management, and administration. The sales compensation process manager will set dates, confirm accountabilities, and oversee the application of the program. This person should never be tasked with the objective to design new plans. Assign this duty to the sales compensation design team and let the process manager manage the process.

SUMMARY

Effective sales compensation design is an inclusive process involving key stakeholders: the CEO/business general manager, vice president of sales, vice president of marketing, and vice president of finance. Staff specialists contribute to the effort by conducting fact finding, analyzing the current plan, gathering external market data, and managing the design process.

Chapter 4

Why Job Content Drives Sales Compensation Design

As we mentioned earlier, sales compensation is driven by sales job content. While industry practices, motivation theory, and company philosophy play contributing roles, the design of a sales compensation plan reflects the type of sales job it supports. In this chapter, we will examine why job content drives sales compensation design. We will look at how different job components combine to form different sales job types. We will then present an inventory of sales jobs. Next, we will look at sales job design errors and how they have a negative impact on sales compensation plan effectiveness. Finally, we will provide examples of sales jobs and their supporting sales compensation elements.

JOB CONTENT DRIVES SALES COMPENSATION DESIGN

Sales compensation is a contributing reason why salespeople want to excel. However, in our view, it is seldom the *primary* reason. Human endeavor is a complex chemistry of intrinsic and extrinsic needs. Leadership models, measurement systems, affiliation variables, and supporting programs (such as the rewards system) contribute to provide the proper direction and motivation to the sales force. Our experience with hundreds of sales forces suggests that beginning with sales job content is a rational and safe starting point for effective sales compensation design. We don't want to preclude alternative approaches or theories. In our view, other variables can explain the existence of unique sales compensation designs but job content can best explain the construct of most sales compensation plans. Perhaps a storyboard will help illustrate how sales compensation design logically flows from job content:

"Okay, Ms. Smith," begins the sales manager. "We have an excellent sales territory for you. You will be calling on small businesses in three zip codes. Your job is to sell telecommunication services to customers already using the major carrier in the market. It's not an easy sell, but we have a great product, superior customer service, and great pricing. Expect a lot of 'Noes,' but don't give up! Now, let me give you an idea of how your compensation package will work. You will receive a commission on all new accounts. You will get a percentage of the revenue for the first 6 months of any new account. After that, the customer will be handled by the customer service team. Although your base salary is low, you have a great upside earning opportunity tied to your sales success."

As this storyboard illustrates, it is almost impossible to split the job content (new account selling) from its supporting sales compensation program (commission on all new sales).

Although most people can list 10 to 15 different types of sales jobs, the list actually totals close to 50 distinct selling jobs. Not all industries or companies use all 50 sales jobs. In fact, it's unlikely that a sales department will use more than 15 or 20 sales jobs and will more likely need only 8 to 12 sales jobs. As we will demonstrate, the foundation of sales compensation design rests with the underlying job content—regardless of the industry or company.

SALES JOB COMPONENTS

In Chapter 1, we presented five components of Sales Process: Demand Creation, Buyer Identification, Purchase Commitment, Order Fulfillment, and Customer Service. Sales organizations need to be "outward facing," supporting different customer populations. In this section, we add two more variables that help further define job content: Customer Segments and Customer Specialization.

- *Customer Segments:* Customer segments include the following categories:
  - *New accounts:* New accounts are prospects that are not current buyers. More narrowly defined segments may identify multiple unique buyers within an account, thus increasing the population of "new" accounts.
  - *Existing accounts:* Existing accounts are current buyers. A company's definition of "former customers" will help correctly assign these returning customers to the right category: "new" or "existing."
  - *Channel partners:* Channel partners represent a vast number of different types of partners who sell products on behalf of the company. Examples include retailers, distributors, value-added resellers, dealers, brokers, agents, and manufacturing representatives. Companies that rely on channel partners deploy indirect sales representatives known as channel representatives to support the channel partners, providing training, promoting product sales, and resolving partner-customer service issues.
  - *Channel end users:* In some cases, the manufacturer will deploy influencing personnel to call on end-user customers. Channel end users create demand for the product and help identify buyers but refer the customer to the channel partner for purchase execution and order fulfillment.

- *Customer Specialization:* Customer specialization includes four major groups of customers:
  - *Stratified:* One of the more popular methods used to group customers is by size. This approach presumes that larger customers have needs different from smaller customers.
  - *Product/Application:* Another method by which to group customers, for sales coverage purposes, is by product or application. In this approach, sales personnel sell a uniform family of products or applications.
  - *Industry:* Certain industries may require specialized sellers knowledgeable about industry issues to properly represent their companies' services.
  - *Geographic:* A final and practical method for specializing customers is by geographic location.

An example of how these various components (process, segments, and specialization) configure into a job can be seen in Figure 4-1. The shading reflects the role of a new account sales representative like Ms. Smith from our storyboard.

Customer Variables		Sales Process				
Segment	Specialization	Demand Creation	Buyer Identification	Purchase Commitment	Order Fulfillment	Customer Service
New Accounts	Stratified					
	Product					
	Industry					
	Geographic	X	X	X	X	
Existing Accounts	Stratified					
	Product					
	Industry					
	Geographic					
Channel Partners	Stratified					
	Product					
	Industry					
	Geographic					
Channel End Users	Stratified					
	Product					
	Industry					
	Geographic					

Figure 4-1 The role of a new account sales representative.

Customer Variables		Sales Process				
Segment	Specialization	Demand Creation	Buyer Identification	Purchase Commitment	Order Fulfillment	Customer Service
New Accounts	Stratified	X	X	X	X	X
	Product					
	Industry					
	Geographic					
Existing Accounts	Stratified		X	X	X	X
	Product					
	Industry					
	Geographic					
Channel Partners	Stratified					
	Product					
	Industry					
	Geographic					
Channel End Users	Stratified					
	Product					
	Industry					
	Geographic					

Figure 4-2 The role of a major account sales representative.

Figure 4-2 shows the role of a major account sales representative.

Figure 4-3 shows sales channel representatives with both channel partner and end-user responsibilities. The sales channel representative sells to the channel partners and promotes purchases to end users, but sales channel representatives do not write end-user orders. In such cases, he or she refers the order to one of the channel partners.

Customer Variables		Sales Process				
Segment	Specialization	Demand Creation	Buyer Identification	Purchase Commitment	Order Fulfillment	Customer Service
New Accounts	Stratified					
	Product					
	Industry					
	Geographic					
Existing Accounts	Stratified					
	Product					
	Industry					
	Geographic					
Channel Partners	Stratified					
	Product	X	X	X		
	Industry					
	Geographic					
Channel End Users	Stratified					
	Product	X	X			
	Industry					
	Geographic					

Figure 4-3 The responsibilities of a sales channel representative.

Figures 4-1 to 4-3 show just how sales process, customer segments, customer specialization, and sales process steps configure into unique sales jobs.

SALES JOB TYPE INVENTORY

The following sales job inventory presents a comprehensive list of sales job types. We have grouped sales jobs into the following six job families:

1. *Income producers:* Income producers define their value as having specialized customer access and typically sell nondifferentiated products.
2. *Direct sales jobs:* Direct sales jobs sell to end users and act as the primary contact to the customer. Direct sellers work either outside the company or are telephone sales personnel. Sales personnel can work for the manufacturer or for a sales channel member such as a distributor, dealer, retailer, or broker.
3. *Indirect sales jobs:* Indirect sales jobs work with partners and other third-party representatives who sell the product on behalf of the manufacturer or service creator.
4. *Overlay sales jobs:* Overlay sales jobs work with, and in support of, the account sales force. They provide additional help to the sales representative.
5. *Business development:* Business development jobs promote and develop market access.
6. *Pre- and postsales support:* These are technical personnel who assist during pre- and/or postsales efforts.

We present the list of jobs for each sales job family next.

Income Producers

Income producers sell other companies' products. However, for the income producer, their true asset is their own loyal customer base.

Agent/broker/ producer	Agents, brokers, and producers are normally dedicated to a single employer. The employers of agents, brokers, and producers do not make products, nor do they purchase (take possession of) the products they sell.
Independent rep	Independent reps are similar to agents, brokers, and producers but are not dedicated to a single employer and may represent noncompetitive products from various manufacturers.
Investment manager	Investment managers provide financial planning advice to investors earning commission income for the sale of investment vehicles.
Multitier marketing rep	Multitier marketing reps sell products and services directly to consumers. Examples include Avon and Amway.
Property development specialist	Property development specialists help arrange real estate investments with payouts occurring before and, sometimes, after distribution or syndication of the investment.
Trader	Traders buy and sell products and earn income by sharing a percentage of the difference between the buy price and the sell price.

Direct Sales Jobs

Direct sales jobs sell to the end user. The company may be the manufacturer or reseller of the product.

Asset manager	Sells to and collaborates with high-revenue customers on a national or worldwide basis.
Channel assignment seller	Advises customers as to the most effective channel to meet their needs. Matriculates the customer in the channel (e.g., convinces customers to use the Web as the preferred purchase channel).
Customer service/ order representative	Accepts inbound calls and books customer orders. No cross-selling or up-selling.
Dealer (showroom)	Sells to customers from showroom floor that presents product for ordering.
Event/project seller	Sells a major project to a customer. No ongoing account responsibility.
Geographic	Sells to assigned accounts within a geographic area.
Geographic—new accounts	Sells to new accounts only within a geographic territory.
Global account	Sells to existing named large customers on a worldwide basis. Does not have local sales resources reports.
Government	Sells to tax-supported entities such as government or military units.
Major account	Sells to a select list of large-name accounts.
Major account (existing)	Sells to a select list of existing, large accounts.
Major account (new)	Sells to a select list of potential, major accounts who are now noncustomers.

Market maker	Sells a new product to noncustomers—creates market for product.
Named account	Sells to an identified list of accounts.
National account	Sells to the headquarters of a major, named customer to secure vendor approval for local selling efforts by others.
Product/service, application	Sells a specific product/service or application within a territory or to assigned accounts.
	Sole owner of the buyer/account.
Referral sales	Sells to new customers via referrals from existing customers.
	No assigned territory, a.k.a. "daisy chain selling."
Renewal	Sells to existing customers' renewal of an existing contract.
Store sales (floor)—retail	Sells from existing floor inventory product (retail).
Telephone account representative	Sells products and services to nonassigned accounts—both inbound and outbound.
Telesales—outbound	Sells products and services to nonassigned accounts on an outbound basis only.
Telesales—inbound	Up-sells and cross-sells on inbound sales opportunities.
Telesales—renewal	Outbound calls to customers with expiring contracts for contract renewal purposes.
	May call on former customers to reestablish contract/service (win-back sellers).

| Vertical/industry | Sells to a specific vertical or industrial market. |
| Win back | Sells to former customers to win back the departed customers. |

The Cost of Overselling Customers. The state Public Utilities Commission (PUC) fined a major telecommunications company millions of dollars for unethical selling practices. Was the incentive plan the cause? Service representatives at phone companies handle customer requests for new phone service, change in service, and billing issues. The state PUC sets billing rates to ensure the phone company offers quality service levels. Telephone companies can earn additional income by selling enhanced services to customers such as call waiting, an extra line, call forwarding, and long-distance services. U.S. border states are popular entry points for recent immigrants. When calling for new phone service, these new immigrants—identified by their accented English—were targeted for packaged solutions loaded with enhanced features at a higher cost. They were not offered the much lower-priced basic service. The PUC identified the incentive plan as the culprit. However, when examined, the incentive could only partially explain the motivation behind this type of predatory selling. The upside earning potential was only 5 percent of base salary, an amount too modest to explain widespread overselling. On further investigation, the source of pressure to oversell customers was not the incentive plan, but supervisors' insistence on hitting the numbers. The supervisors were under significant pressure to grow revenues.

Preferred Solution: Recharter the customer service model to meet customer needs first. Retrain supervisors. Use other sales channels to promote enhanced products other than overselling on inbound service calls. (Of interest, it was employees—the service representatives—who alerted the PUC about the abusive selling tactics that were being foisted on them by their supervisors.)

Indirect Sales Jobs

Indirect sellers work with sales channel partners and other third parties who sell products to end users. Indirect sellers do not sell to end users; the channel partner is responsible for the sale.

Channel end-user representative	Works with end-user customers to promote products that are purchased from channel partners. Works with assigned channel partners.
Channel representative	Promotes products to channel partner, who resells products to customers. Works with channel member sales personnel of channel partners such as value-added resellers (VARs), retailers, distributors, brokers, and independent software vendors (ISVs). May also call on end users to help promote channel partner sales.
HQ sales-in (retail)	Sells products to the headquarters of retail chains.
Influence seller	Promotes products to influencers who can specify product purchase; examples of such purchase influencers include doctors, consultants, engineers, and architects.
In-store sales-out	Works in retail outlets to place and/or promote company products. Sometimes referred to as merchandisers.

Jobber	Restocks customer products at retail locations.
	May promote product placement.
Original equipment manufacturer (OEM)	Sells products (e.g., components, seller subsystems) to manufacturers that incorporate into a final manufactured product.

Overlay Sales Jobs

Overlay sales jobs work in support of direct sales jobs and, occasionally, indirect sales jobs to provide additional sales support to the primary seller.

Application specialist	An application specialist has an in-depth knowledge of a specific application or family of applications.
	Assists the assigned seller to help promote the application to customers or channel partners.
Product specialist	A product specialist has an in-depth knowledge of a select product or family of products.
	Assists the assigned seller to help promote the product to customers or channel partners.
Service specialist	A service specialist has an in-depth knowledge of a select service or family of services.
	Assists the assigned seller to help promote the service to the customer or channel partner.

Vertical specialist   A vertical specialist has an in-depth knowledge of a specific industry or buyer type.

Assists assigned sellers to help promote the company's products or services to a specific vertical/industry market.

Business Development

A business development resource promotes the company's products and services to emerging market opportunities with customers or channel partners. These individuals usually do not have sales goals but are given management by objective (MBO)–type measures.

Alliance/joint venture specialist   Alliance/joint venture specialist establishes company's alliance and joint venture partnership efforts.

May or may not manage ongoing relationship.

End-user channel representative   End-user channel representative calls on end users to stimulate product sales but refers sales opportunities to sanctioned channel partner.

Not dedicated to supporting any channel partner.

New channel developer   New channel developer recruits new channel partners.

New offering specialist   New offering specialist presents the company's product and service to customers to test customer interest, confirm the value proposition, and identify the preferred market segments.

Pre- and Postsales Support

Pre- and postsales technical support are not considered sales personnel but are often an integral part of the selling effort. They have customer contact and frequently influence the customer to act; however, a direct or indirect salesperson owns the account and the pre- and postsales support person works at the salesperson's direction.

Postsales technical support	Works with sales personnel to help install, adopt, and implement the purchased solution.
Pre- and postsales technical support	Works with sales personnel on both pre- and postsales technical issues.
Presales technical support	Works with sales personnel to facilitate the sales to customers. Provides technical support including interpretation, need requirements, and solution configuration.

The above job inventory presents more than 50 different sales jobs. We assume there are more jobs than this. However, these are the most prevalent and represent over 90 percent of all sellers. Each company may provide a unique name for the job, but regardless of the title, most jobs can be matched based on their content to one of the job types listed previously.

JOB LEVELS

Job levels reflect the gradation of impact, experience, and defined importance of the job. The higher the level, the greater the expected output of the incumbent and, correspondingly, the greater the target total cash compensation for a job. Progression from one job level to the next is a reward for individual performance. Level titles vary significantly from industry to industry and company to company. For example, the title of vice president might be given to high-level sales personnel in the banking industry whereas a similar job might be called a sales executive in a high-technology company. Normally, job levels can be broken down into four generic levels:

1. *Associate:* A sales associate is a common title for an entry-level sales job. It denotes the lowest job level on the organization chart.
2. *Representative:* A sales representative is a fully trained salesperson accountable for his or her actions and assigned responsibilities.
3. *Senior representative:* A senior sales representative is a seasoned sales representative. He or she will most likely have the same job content as a sales representative but will have proved him- or herself with demonstrated, sustained, productive performance over a period of time. Often given more autonomy than a representative, this position usually has the highest head count in a well-configured sales department.
4. *Account executive:* An account executive is the most senior sales level requiring advanced selling and customer skills. The account executive may act as an individual seller or coordinate (lead) the efforts of other sellers too.

Each of the 50-plus jobs listed above could, conceivably, have all four job levels, thus increasing the number of distinct sales and sales-like jobs to over 200.

JOB DESIGN ERRORS

As mentioned earlier, sales compensation follows job design. One of the challenges facing sales strategists is to design and deploy effective sales jobs. An effective sales job has focus, clarity of purpose, and a clearly identified point of persuasion responsibility. While the point of persuasion should be the primary focus, sometimes multiple constraints often (and sometimes, correctly) compromise this singular focus.

- *Costs:* Although we would like to have sales personnel focus all their time on selling activities and let others do the customer service work, the cost to hire others to perform such nonselling tasks may not be plausible. Therefore, the salesperson may find that other customer-related tasks will displace selling time.
- *Customer expectations:* An unhappy customer is not inclined to make additional purchases from a salesperson. Therefore, the salesperson must shift from selling activities to customer service responsibilities in order to improve the customer's current satisfaction before returning to pure selling efforts.
- *Product or service configuration:* Sometimes the product or service configuration precludes exclusive focus on selling. For example, in some services, the seller is expected to also deliver the solution, as in the case of custom training or consulting.

However, the best sales forces will continually adjust sales job content to ensure that focus of the job is at the point of persuasion. The following is a list of the four most common sales job design errors:

- *Sales job design error 1: the corrupted sales:* Sometimes referred to as a contaminated sales job. Responsibilities of other departments have crept into the selling job, such as collections, marketing, and customer service.
- *Sales job design error 2: the blended sales job:* Sales jobs function best when they have a single focus. Focus occurs when the goals are few and the cadence is uniform. Too many goals overwhelm the focus of a sales job. This can occur when the seller is given several selling tasks to undertake at one time: "Sell new business, sell to existing customers, and work with channel partners." Each

of these tasks is vital and warranted but when combined into the same job, the result is a blended job with too many goals. Blended sales jobs can also erode sales cadence—the rhythm of activity. Selling to the major customer has a long sales cycle while selling to new, smaller customers may have a very short sales cycle. In this case, the cadences of the two sales jobs are at odds with each other, contributing to the blended job design error.

- *Sales job design error 3: bandwidth exceeded:* Another job design error begins with good intentions but often produces a third error in job design: too many products and too many dissimilar customers for the salesperson to handle. Today's electronic sales support has given sales forces more bandwidth but there is a limit to the breadth of products and customers that a salesperson can manage. Overloading a sales job will cause the incumbents to start ignoring elements of the product and customer mix.

- *Sales job design error 4: undetected job transformation:* Although not a true job design error, some jobs transform from an initial job to a new, different job. Same person, same sales territory, and same accounts, but the first job (open new accounts) transforms upon success into a second job (manage the base of business). While this is a preferred business outcome, sometimes the measurement and reward systems do not transform at the same time to match the new, evolved job. The result is a misalignment between job content selling tactics.

Sales management needs to rectify sales job design errors prior to drafting sales compensation plans.

SALES COMPENSATION PRACTICES BY JOB TYPES

Figure 4-4 provides examples of different pay mixes, leverages, and measures by job type. These are sample illustrations of how sales job content affects pay plans.

Job Type	Title	Mix and Leverage	Measures
Income Producers	Agent	N/A	Commission on All Sales
	Independent Rep	N/A	Commission on All Sales
Direct Sales Representatives	Asset Manager	80/20, 2.5x	Return on Sales
	Geographic Rep	60/40, 3.5x	All Sales
	Major Account Rep	75/25, 3x	Sales and Retention
	Telesales Inbound	80/20, 3x	Up-sell, Cross-sell
	Telesales Outbound	50/50, 3x	New Sales
	Vertical Rep	70/30, 3x	Vertical Sales
Indirect Sales Representatives	Channel Rep	75/25, 3x	Sales and Channel Balance
	OEM Seller	70/30, 3x	New Placements
Overlay Specialist	Application Specialist	80/20, 2.5x	Sales and New Accounts
	Product Specialist	80/20, 2.5x	Sales and Rep Balance
Business Development	Alliance Specialist	100/0 +25%	New Alliances MBO
	Channel End User	90/10, 2.5x	Sell Through
Technical Support	Presales Tech Support	90/10, 2.5x	District Sales
	Postsales Tech Support	100/0 +10%	District Sales

Figure 4-4 Job type and pay plan design.

SUMMARY

Our experience has shown that when sales compensation plans become ineffective, it is usually because the plans attempt to fix a job design mistake. In particular, be on the lookout for corrupted and blended sales jobs. A sales compensation project always examines job content for clarity and focus.

Chapter 5

Formula Types

At the core of every sales compensation plan is a formula that translates sales performance into income for the salesperson. This chapter presents a comprehensive listing of the different types of sales compensation formulas. Each formula is effective given the proper job context. In other words, these formulas are neither good nor bad, but can be effective or ineffective depending on their job application.

TYPES OF PLANS

In Chapter 2, we introduced five different types of incentive plans. In this chapter we will present formulas for Unit Rate plans and for Target Pay plans, including 3×, 2×, and Add-on plans. Companies seldom use Gainsharing plans for sales personnel unless part of an all-employee companywide plan. See Figure 5-1 for the different types of variable compensation plans.

ILLUSTRATING FORMULA PAYOUTS WITH SALES COMPENSATION FORMULA GRAPHS

To facilitate our presentation of the incentive compensation formula types, we will use a popular convention for presenting sales compensation designs: the sales compensation formula graph. The sales

Types of Variable Compensation Plans

Figure 5-1 Types of variable compensation plans.

compensation formula graph presents a visual representation of the pay formula. We present several pay formula types using this graph. Figure 5-2 presents the basic construction of the formula graph.

Note: A compensation graph always displays compensation (pay) on the vertical (*y* axis) and sales production on the horizontal (*x* axis).

Figure 5-3 provides notations with callouts printed on the formula graph. The two callouts show the first and second commission rates. From a mathematical perspective, the *commission rate* is the slope or the relationship between compensation and performance.

Figure 5-2 Compensation formula graph.

Figure 5-3 Compensation formula graph with commission rates.

TWO MAJOR SELLER CATEGORIES

As described earlier, there are two major categories of sales jobs: income producers and sales representatives. The underlying economic foundation for each differs from the other. Income producers share a percent of the revenue, whereas sales representatives earn incentive payments as a portion of a predetermined target earnings amount. While both seller categories share many of the same mathematical formula mechanics, the basis of pay is profoundly different. Income producers have shared ownership of the sales results, regardless of earning level, either low or high. Conversely, sales representatives earn a portion of a target incentive amount. In this respect, the company's commitment and obligation are to the target earning opportunity and not to a percent of the revenue. For sales representatives, management determines what level of performance warrants what level of incentive pay. For income producers, the seller's production times the commission rate determines pay levels without regard to a target earning amount.

UNIT RATE PLANS

In this section, we will examine Unit Rate plans. Unit Rate plans, sometimes called straight commission plans, provide a payment per transaction. Management uses these designs to reward income producers.

The pay mechanics for income producers is relatively easy to present. Since income producers are "the business," they receive a share of each sales unit, for example, payment per sales revenue dollar or payment per unit sold. There are various types of Unit Rate plans.

We present the following Unit Rate income producer plans, which we will refer to as Plans 1 to 5:

1. Flat Commission
2. Ramped Commission
3. Residuals/Trailing/Back-End Payouts
4. Pool
5. Override

1. Unit Rate: Flat Commission

The flat commission schedule, shown in Figure 5-4, is the simplest of all sales compensation formulas. The formula provides a percent of sales dollar for each dollar of sales production or payment for each unit sold. Here are examples of flat commission plans:

Example 1: 6% commission paid for all sales dollars
Example 2: 25% commission paid on all gross margin dollars
Example 3: $10 commission paid for each unit sold

Figure 5-4 Unit rate plan 1: flat commission.

Note: In the example in Figure 5-4, payment begins with the first dollar or unit of sale. So there is no threshold that must be reached before payments can begin; nor is there a cap or maximum payment either. In this illustration, commission earnings are unlimited.

Observations

A flat commission, with no base salary, is a very powerful and focused pay program. Expect the income producer sales force to look primarily to the pay program for direction and focus.

Vocabulary Alert: Flat commission and straight commission are different. The term *flat commission* means a constant or unchanging rate. Straight commission represents a different concept. The term *straight commission* means no base salary where all earnings are achieved through the sales compensation program. The following sentence correctly illustrates this usage: The compensation program features a straight commission with no base salary; the flat commission formula pays the same rate on all sales production.

2. Unit Rate: Ramped Commission

While the flat commission formula does not change, a ramped commission schedule has more than one commission rate. A progressive ramp formula, shown in Figure 5-5, features a second

Figure 5-5 Unit rate plan 2: ramped commission—progressive.

Component	Progressive Ramp Commission Schedule		
Commission Rate		**Sales Performance**	**Commission Rate**
	1st Commission Rate	To $1M	6%
	2nd Commission Rate	$1M and Over	8%

Figure 5-6 Progressive ramp commission schedule.

commission rate higher than the first commission rate, sometimes known as an "accelerator."

In Figure 5-5, we see that the commission rate increases after the first $1 million in performance. Figure 5-6 shows the commission formula for a ramped commission schedule.

Observations

A progressive ramp commission formula has all the motivation of a flat commission plan. Use this approach when more sales are difficult, but very desirable to the company.

3. Unit Rate: Residuals/Trailing/Back-End Payouts

For most income producers, the incentive formula continues to pay as long as the revenue continues. For example, life insurance premiums continue on an annual basis. In some cases, these commission payments might decline. Figure 5-7 is an example of a declining

Component	Residual Commission Schedule	
	Insurance Premium Residuals	
Commission Rate	**Year of Policy**	**Portion of Annual Premium**
	1	100%
	2	75%
	3	25%
	4	0%

Figure 5-7 Declining residual commission schedule.

residual commission schedule. The value of the recurring revenue has value but on a declining basis, eventually providing no income to the salesperson by the fourth year.

As an income producer, the pay program usually assures these future earnings unless abridged by the payment policy. In some instances, there is a buyout provision to make payments on these future earnings if the income producer should leave while revenue continues. "Trailing" is another expression for residuals.

In other cases, the commission plan does not make full payments until the disposition of an investment such as real estate. Back-end payouts are common in property and real estate development when the true value of the deal is not realized until the investment and/or property is sold at some future date. As specified in the compensation plan, the income producer will earn a percent of profits (normally) when the investors sell, syndicate, liquidate, or transfer the property.

Observations

Paying for future revenue or profits is the annuity element of income producer plans.

4. Unit Rate: Pool

A pool plan creates a block of money for distribution to participants. Normally, a percent of revenue or profit generates the pool funds. Use pool payments for income producers who cross-share realized income. For example, traders (currency, bonds, electrical power, and many others) often work on a trading floor as part of a work unit.

The incentive plan for traders would split the trading profits into two payments. The first portion goes to the individual trader; the second portion into the pool. The pool distributes these dollars at the end of the performance period by a predefined formula, as illustrated in Figure 5-8.

Component	Traders' Pool
Individual Commission	75% of the trading earnings is paid to the trader
Traders' Pool	25% of all trading earnings are accumulated in the Traders' Pool

Title	Portion of Traders' Pool
Senior Traders	50%—divided equally
Traders	35%—divided equally
Trading Assistants	15%—divided equally

Figure 5-8 Traders' pool.

Some organizations use a hybrid individual and pool model. One hybrid approach features a commission paid to individuals for normal transactions and the earnings for mega deals partially allocated to a pool for distribution at the end of the performance period. Another hybrid approach is to accumulate the pool based on performance, but allow manager judgment of individual contribution to affect some or all of the pool payout to participants.

Observations

Pools are not widely used except for certain trading and financial markets. Pools are not effective at driving (causing) team performance. They are primarily a mechanism for sharing results.

> **Vocabulary Alert:** *Participation rate* is a term often used for income producers to define their share of the income. While this is the same idea as a commission rate, the implicit sense of ownership is reaffirmed by the use of the phrase *participation rate,* implying a *shared* ownership in the results—a concept consistent with incentive compensation plans for income producers.

5. Unit Rate: Override

Multilevel marketing uses the concepts of overrides in a correct and positive fashion. Each person earns commissions on sales of their

Component	Override Commission
Override Commission	Percent of Subordinates' Commissions **Subordinates Commission** **Rate** To $2.5M 5% $2.5M and Over 9%

Figure 5-9 Override commission schedule.

recruited subordinates known as a "network." The more sellers recruited, the more money earned through override payments.

An override provides a proportional commission payment to the supervisor. With large distribution networks with several layers of sellers, supervisors and managers earn a commission override from all the levels below them.

Figure 5-9 displays an example of a commission override formula.

Observations

Multilevel marketers generally promote high energy and positive thinking but suffer high turnover. Individuals have the potential to earn substantial income by building effective high-populated networks. Seller costs are fully variable but long-term commitment is fleeting.

Unit Rate Plans Summary

Income producers are sellers who control (own) their accounts. The product they sell is usually a commodity and is, therefore, undifferentiated. The value of the business is the contacts and relationships of the seller with his or her customers. Normally, income producers arrive with a book of business and when they leave might keep over 80 percent of their accounts. Income producer commission plans pay a percent of the sales production. Funding for the incentive comes from sales results. Commission rates define competitive market rates, not actual dollars earned.

Sales representative compensation differs from income producers' pay. Instead of providing a competitive commission rate as they do for income producers, sales management identifies a target pay amount for sales representative jobs. Sales management then develops a formula to ensure expected performance achieves this target payout amount. Formulas differ depending on the sales objective assigned by the company. Compensation professionals will judge competitiveness for sales representative compensation plans by actual payouts as compared to the preferred market-driven target pay amount. Income producers simply use the market commission rate (unit rate) to judge competitiveness of the plan. Payouts are the outcome of performance, not a stated competitive objective.

Without close examination, it's easy to misclassify a sales representative as an income producer, and, therefore, provide an inappropriate pay program. We estimate that sales representatives account for over 90 percent of all sellers, while the remaining 10 percent are income producers.

TARGET PAY INCENTIVE PLANS: COMMISSION VERSUS BONUS

Sales representatives sell a unique offering created by the company. The value to the customer is the company's products and services and not the salesperson. Companies manage sales representatives' pay to a target incentive amount. For performance below goal, the pay is less than the target incentive amount. For performance above goal, the incentive payment is above the target incentive amount.

When building a compensation program for income producers, start with a commission rate. When building a sales compensation program for sales representatives, begin with a target incentive amount. The purpose of target pay incentive plans is to manage the earning opportunity for sales personnel.

There are other significant implications when using target pay incentive plans:

- *Earnings commitment:* For income producers, the company commits to the commission percentage. For sales representatives, the company makes a commitment to the target earnings opportunity.
- *Funding:* Funding for income producers' commissions comes from revenue production. For sales representatives, incentive compensation is cross-funded by the plan participants. The incentive plan for sales representatives reallocates target pay among the participants with better performers making more than the target incentive and less effective performers making less than the target pay.

Target Pay Calculation Engines: Commission versus Bonus

There are many formula methods for calculating the sales compensation payments for sales representatives. These formula methods fall into two major groupings: target incentive commission formula (TI-Commission) and target incentive bonus formula (TI-Bonus). In both cases, the construction of the incentive formula begins with identifying a target incentive amount. Depending on territory size variance, use either a commission formula or a bonus formula to calculate payouts of the target incentive.

A TI-Commission plan looks very much like the commission schedule used for income producers. The formula expresses the payout as a percent of sales results or payment per unit. However, while the formula constructs look almost identical to those used for income producers, the underlying design assumptions are very different. Sales representative plan designs begin with a target pay amount reserved for those who achieve target performance. Each sales representative job title has a target pay level. Assuming that the territories are of equal potential, calculate a commission rate to ensure that sales representatives earn target incentive pay for target performance.

The formula for calculating a commission rate is as follows:

$$\frac{\text{Target Incentive Amount}}{\text{Target Volume}} \times 100 = \text{Commission Rate}$$

Or, as an illustration:

$$\frac{\$100,000}{\$2,000,000} \times 100 = 5\% \text{ Commission Rate}$$

TI-Bonus plans earn a percent of target incentive earnings for performance as compared to quota. Use the TI-Bonus formula when territories are not of equal size but you wish to provide similar earnings opportunities. Whether the territory is $1M or $2M, $5M or $10M, accomplishment of sales objectives can be expressed as a percent of goal: 75 percent of goal, 100 percent of goal, or 125 percent of goal, for example. In this manner, the formula expresses payments as a percent of goal achieved and not as a percent of absolute dollars. The outcome of this approach is to provide similar earnings opportunities for dissimilar-sized territories. The TI-Bonus formula manages payouts in relation to quota, regardless of the absolute size of the territories. Figure 5-10 presents an example of the TI-Bonus formula.

Component	Bonus Formula—Step-Based	
	Step-Based TI-Bonus Formula	
	Percent to Quota	**Percent of Target Incentive**
	Over 125%	150%
Bonus	110% to 124%	125%
Schedule	105% to 109%	110%
	100% to 104%	100%
	90% to 99%	75%
	80% to 89%	50%
	Below 80%	0%

Figure 5-10 TI-bonus formula—step-based.

Table 5-1 Summary of TI-Bonus Formula Payouts by Employee

Employee	Territory Actual dollar	Percent quota	Target incentive
A	$1.50M	100%	$35,000
B	$1.75M	100%	$35,000
C	$1.25M	100%	$35,000
D	$3.00M	100%	$35,000
E	$2.58M	100%	$35,000

In this case, the TI-Bonus formula makes payouts regardless of actual size of the territory. As shown in Table 5-1, for example, 100 percent of quota can differ by employee, but the target incentive remains the same; thus equalizing the earning opportunities among territories.

In summary, use the TI-Commission formula when sales territories have similar revenue opportunities. When sales territories do not have equal revenue potential, use the TI-Bonus formula. In Chapter 6, we will learn how to calculate commission (and bonus) schedules.

SALES REPRESENTATIVE OR MARKETING REPRESENTATIVE?

Some field customer contact jobs appear to be those of sales representatives but are, in fact, marketing jobs. If the field person is executing a brand strategy such as providing product displays or training channel sales personnel without any influencing role, then the job might be a marketing job. Marketing jobs can be eligible for add-on incentives, but not sales compensation.

TARGET INCENTIVE PLANS: COMMISSION FORMULA

The following are sales representative Target Incentive (TI)-Commission sample plans, which we refer to as Plans 6–20. These plans assume that territories are approximately equal in revenue opportunity.

6. Commission—Flat
7. Commission—Ramped Progressive
8. Commission—Ramped Regressive
9. Commission—Ramped, Progressive and Regressive
10. Commission—Ramped with Base Salary
11. Commission—With Limits
12. Variable Commission—Product Rates
13. Variable Commission—Value Table
14. Variable Commission—Product Points
15. Variable Commission—Profit Variance
16. Linked Commission—With Hurdle
17. Linked Commission—Product Rates with Hurdle
18. Linked Commission—With Multiplier
19. Linked Commission—With Matrix
20. Commission—For Stratified Sales Force

6. TI: Commission—Flat

Similar to the Flat Commission plan for income producers, the target incentive flat commission (see Figure 5-11) is the simplest sales

Figure 5-11 Flat commission—no base salary.

Component	Flat Commission Schedule		
Commission Rate	Commission Rate	**Sales Performance** All Sales	**Commission Rate** 7%

Figure 5-12 Flat commission schedule.

compensation for a target incentive formula. We have made only a slight modification. The term "target compensation" confirms a target pay design. This Target Incentive (TI)-commission rate is a function of the target incentive divided by the target sales production to determine the TI-commission rate.

A sample formula for a flat commission program is given in Figure 5-12.

In this example, there is no threshold and no cap. This formula type assumes that territories have relatively equal potential. Often sales management will realign territories or accounts to balance the potential. Use of a TI-commission becomes less plausible when the difference between the smallest territory and the largest territory becomes greater by a factor of $2\times$.

Observations

Straight commission plans (no base salary) are not common for sales representatives, although sales management might use such a plan for a high-influence sales job where sales management needs fully variable costs and high turnover is acceptable.

7. TI: Commission—Ramped Progressive

Progressive ramp commission rates (see Figure 5-13) provide added motivation for selling beyond target. In a progressive ramp, the second rate is higher than the first rate. The new rate is only effective when the target amount is reached and does not

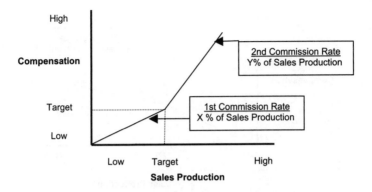

Figure 5-13 Commission—progressive ramp.

(should not) "retro-back" to pay the previous sales volume at the new, higher rate.

Figure 5-14 is an illustration of a ramped commission schedule.

In this example, we see that the commission rate increases from 6 percent to 8 percent. A predetermined level of accomplishment is achieved—in this case $1.5M.

Observations

Most incentive formulas feature a progressive ramp. This approach rewards additional sales performance.

8. TI: Commission—Ramped Regressive

In some instances, the commission rate declines at a predetermined level. Sales representatives do not view regressive rates favorably. However, in some instances the company needs to avoid excessive

Component	Progressive Ramp Commission Schedule		
		Sales Performance	**Commission Rate**
Commission Rate	1st Commission Rate	To $1.5M	6%
	2nd Commission Rate	Over $1.5M	8%

Figure 5-14 Progressive ramp commission schedule.

Figure 5-15 Commission—ramped regressive.

upside payments caused by either poor quota setting or unexpected windfalls. Figure 5-15 displays a regressive ramp rate.

Figure 5-16 is an illustration of a regressive ramp commission schedule.

In this example, we see that the commission rate decreases from 7 percent to 5 percent at a predetermined level—in this case, $2M.

Observations

As with any regressive plan, not paying more for additional sales seems de-motivational, to salespeople. Yet, most sales personnel understand the logic of a regressive formula, even though they do not like it. However, regressive formulas do present a communication challenge for sales management.

Component	Regressive Ramp Commission Schedule		
Commission Rate		Sales Performance	Commission Rate
	1st Commission Rate	To $2.0M	7%
	2nd Commission Rate	Over $2.0M	5%

Figure 5-16 Regressive ramp commission schedule.

Figure 5-17 Commission—ramped, progressive and regressive.

9. TI: Commission—Ramped, Progressive and Regressive

In this hybrid example (see Figure 5-17), we see the use of both progressive and regressive ramps.

Figure 5-18 is an illustration of a hybrid progressive/regressive ramp commission schedule.

Observations

The hybrid approach uses both the positive (progressive) and negative (regressive) motivation impact of ramps. It provides additional rewards for additional sales, but after reaching a predetermined point, the commission rate declines.

10. TI: Commission—Ramped with Base Salary

Straight commission plans feature pay plans with no base salary. The incentive formula provides all the earnings. Figure 5-19 illustrates

Component	Commission—Ramped Progressive and Regressive		
		Sales Performance	Commission Rate
Commission Rate	1st Commission Rate (x)	To $2.4M	4%
	2nd Commission Rate (y)	$2.5M–$5.0M	7%
	3rd Commission Rate (z)	Over $5.0M	5%

Figure 5-18 Ramped progressive and regressive commission schedule.

Figure 5-19 Commission—ramped with base salary.

commission with a base salary. The sales representative earns a commission on top of the base salary. The addition of target base salary and target incentive for the job defines the total target cash compensation assigned to the job.

Figure 5-20 is an illustration of base salary with a progressive ramp commission schedule.

Observations

A regressive incentive formula will continue to challenge sales personnel. Management must explain why a regressive formula both protects the company and the employee. Sales personnel still earn additional monies, particularly on mega orders that the alternative cap plan would preclude.

Component	Commission Ramped with Base Salary			
Part 1: Base Salary	**Base Salary/Year** $55,000			
Part 2: Commission Rate	1st Commission Rate 2nd Commission Rate	**Sales** **Performance** To $2.0M Over $2.0M	**Commission** **Rate** 4% 7%	

Figure 5-20 Base salary and ramped commission schedule.

Figure 5-21 TI-Commission—with limits.

11. TI-Commission—with Limits

In Figure 5-21, we see the application of a threshold and a cap. We will learn how and when to use thresholds and caps later in this chapter.

Figure 5-22 is an illustration of a base salary with a progressive ramp commission schedule (with threshold and maximum).

Observations

In addition to a base salary, this plan features a commission plan with both a threshold and a maximum. There is no payment for performance below threshold and no payment for performance

Component	Commission Schedule with Limits		
<u>Part 1:</u> Base Salary	<u>Base Salary/Year</u> $45,000		
<u>Part 2:</u> Commission Rate		**Sales <u>Performance</u>**	**Commission <u>Rate</u>**
	To Threshold	$1.24	0%
	1st Commission Rate	$1.25M to $2.4M	7%
	2nd Commission Rate	$2.5M over $3.0M	9%
	Maximum	Over $3.0M	0%

Figure 5-22 TI-Commission schedule—with limits.

above the maximum. While there are numerous reasons to use both thresholds and caps, the following are the most common:

- *Thresholds:* The primary reason for using a threshold is to avoid re-paying a sales event that occurred in previous years, even though the revenue may be continuing. Do not treat ongoing revenue from a previous sale as an annuity. In such cases, the threshold is set at or above assured recurring revenue. There are other reasons for using a threshold. First, some organizations believe salespeople should "cover" their base salaries prior to earning the first incentive dollar. Second, some organizations want to motivate the salesperson to achieve a minimum level of quota performance. The threshold ensures that performance is consistent with this objective. Finally, other sales organizations simply use a threshold as a statement of management intent of what is the minimum level of acceptable performance.
- *Maximums:* Maximums (or caps) have always been problematic for sales organizations. Most sales forces view maximums as de-motivational. But companies use maximums for a number of reasons. The most common reason is to preclude excessive earnings for unexpected, large orders. And another reason is to protect against excessive earnings due to unaggressive, low quotas. Although sales management should avoid the use of maximums, their use is necessary in certain cases. Use caps when excessive sales are detrimental to the company's production capacity, or when sales personnel could achieve extraordinary sales results through unscrupulous sales practices.

12. TI: Variable Commission—Product Rates

Variable commission plans provide different commission rates for different objectives. The most common form of a variable commission plan is to provide separate commission rates for different

Figure 5-23 Variable rate commission.

product categories where certain products earn a high commission rate and others do not. This variation in commission rates helps guide sales representatives to the most preferred sales outcome. Figure 5-23 is an example of a variable commission plan with two different commission rates by Products A and B.

In Figure 5-24, the two commission rates provide separate payouts depending on the product.

Observations

Variable commission rates assume that sales personnel can influence the customers' buying preference among products.

13. TI: Variable Commission—Value Table

The value table (see Figure 5-25) provides another form of variable commission programs. The variable commission table changes the

Component	Variable Commission—Product Rates		
		Sales **Performance**	**Commission** **Rate**
Commission Rates	Commission Rate "X"	Product A	4%
	Commission Rate "Z"	Product B	2%

Figure 5-24 Variable commission—product rates.

Component	Variable Commission—Value Table		
Product Table	Adjustment to sales dollars: **Adjustment Factor** Product ABC 50% Product Blue 110% Product Red 90% All New Account Sales 125% Commission rates applied to summation of the adjusted sales dollars.		
Commission Rates		**Performance to Goal**	**Commission Rate**
	1st Commission Rate	To 100%	6%
	2nd Commission Rate	Above 100%	8%

Figure 5-25 Variable commission—value table.

economic value of each sales dollar prior to applying the appropriate commission rate. The value table increases or decreases the value of each sale for compensation purposes depending on the product category. For example, a product category that has an adjustment factor of 50 percent would treat the economic value of a $100,000 sale as $50,000 for compensation purposes.

Observations

The value table is similar to variable commission rates. In both cases, the value of revenue dollars for incentive purposes change based on important strategic objectives. The value table provides more flexibility to alter the value of numerous selling objectives at the same time.

14. TI: Variable Commission—Product Points

A product point incentive plan provides different points for each dollar of sale. Figure 5-26 presents different product points for each product. This encourages the sales of valuable, important, or difficult-to-sell products. The point schedule changes the economic value of sale by awarding points depending on strategic

Component	Variable Commission—Product Points		
Point Schedule	Points awarded for each dollar sold: Premium Products Deluxe Products Standard Products Distributed Products	**Points/Dollar** 15 10 5 3	
Conversion Rates	Summation of points times conversion rate. Each point equals: 1st Conversion Rate 2nd Conversion Rate	**Performance to Goal** To 100% Above 100%	**Conversion Rate** 25 Cents/point 35 Cents/point

Figure 5-26 Variable commission—product points.

intent of the product. The payout schedule converts the points to dollars.

This approach, popular with product managers, allows for the frequent fine-tuning of the sales compensation program to achieve strategic product objectives. Management can make adjustments to the table values from one performance period to another.

Observations

All variable adjustment methods share the same strengths and weaknesses. On the positive side, they allow the weighting of key products or sales objectives. This provides a means for management to focus efforts. It allows sales force discretion to sell what the customer needs, yet helps promote products that are strategically important to the company. The negative side of such systems is as follows:

- Such programs require a separate revenue recognition accounting system, different than the real dollars the company earns.
- There is a tendency by sales personnel to "shop-the-plan" or look for the right combination of market needs and their own sales proficiency. This may or may not meet the company's

Component	Variable Commission—Profit Variance	
Commission Rates	**Percent of Gross Margin Dollars**	
	Order GP Percent	**Commission Rate**
	45%	35%
	35% to 44%	33%
	25% to 34%	30%
	15% to 24%	20%
	5% to 14%	8%
	Less than 5%	0%

Figure 5-27 Variable commission—profit variance incentive schedule.

needs. Too many choices tend to dilute the directional impact of value adjustment programs.

15. TI: Variable Commission—Profit Variance

When sales personnel have pricing flexibility, it might be necessary to entice the salesperson to achieve higher pricing. For distributors, who measure gross margin dollars and gross margin percent, an incentive schedule such as the one displayed in Figure 5-27 provides higher commission rates for higher gross profit (GP) percent.

Observations

Incentive plans that link commission rates to profitability can help lift pricing. For manufacturing companies who create products, the best measure of profitability is price-realization. Distributors use gross profit/margin percent.

ABOUT LINK DESIGNS

Link designs are one of the most advanced formula techniques available. Sometimes known as linkages, they tie incentive payouts to the outcomes of two or more performance measures. These linkages do not always create additive payouts. Instead, linkages can provide both a positive impact on the upside of performance and a negative impact on the downside of performance.

There are three types of link formulas:

- *Hurdles:* As with all linkages, hurdles link two or more measures. A hurdle requires the salesperson to accomplish measure A before realizing the beneficial payout related to measure B. For example, "No ramp commission rate will be paid on product A unless the sales performance for product B exceeds 50 percent of goal."
- *Multipliers:* Multipliers tie measures together in a mathematical formula. The incentive value of the first measure is either increased or decreased depending on the performance of the second measure. In this manner, the seller knows the incentive plan can change the economic gain of the first measure by performance on the second measure. For example, "The commission earnings from the core product will be increased or decreased based on the percent to quota sales performance on the second measure of product mix."
- *Matrices:* A matrix is another form of a link design. A matrix features two measures in a grid with rows and columns. The better the performance on both measures, the better the reward.

Linkages reward balanced sales efforts by rewarding the salesperson for achieving all sales objectives.

16. TI: Linked Commission—with Hurdle

A sales compensation plan with a hurdle provides differentiated payouts for a first measure depending on how well the seller performs on a second measure (see Figure 5-28).

Figure 5-28 Linked commission—with hurdle.

Figure 5-29 illustrates a commission rate schedule featuring a hurdle.

The commission schedule of a linked hurdle features different payout rates depending on achieving the hurdle measure.

Observations

A hurdle provides focus to sales efforts. Outstanding performance without meeting the hurdle has a significant downside impact. Likewise, achieving the hurdle has a significant positive upside impact.

Component	Linked Commission—With Hurdle		
Commission Rate	**Hurdle:** Sales of Product XYZ must be at 80% of quota or higher for all revenue on all products to receive the accelerated commission rate of 6%.		
		Hurdle Performance	
		Below Hurdle	**At or Above Hurdle**
	Commission Rate	4%	6%
	If hurdle is not met, the commission schedule pays the below-hurdle rate of 4% on all revenue.		

Figure 5-29 Commission rate schedule with hurdle.

> **Vocabulary Alert.** While the two phrases *threshold* and *hurdle* sound alike, they are not the same. A threshold is a minimum level of performance for one measure that must be achieved before payments are earned on that measure. A hurdle ties the payout of one measure to performance accomplishment on a second measure. Here is an application of these words: "You must meet the *threshold* of the quota before any payout can be earned." "Your commission earnings on all sales will be increased 10 percent if you meet or exceed the weighted average 35 percent gross margin *hurdle*."

17. TI: Linked Commission—Product Rates with Hurdle

Figure 5-30 is an example of a commission plan with variable product rates and a product balance hurdle. While the payout schedule is not capped, the upside commission rates are not available unless the hurdle is met.

Observations

Hurdles are easy to understand. One limitation is that they are like an on/off switch. Either the sales representative reaches the hurdle or not. This can cause a major reduction in pay for only a minimal level of underperformance.

Component	Linked Variable Commission—Product Rates With Hurdle		
Commission Rate	**Hurdle:** All products must be at 75% of quota before the second commission rate on any product becomes available.		
		Product Categories	
		Digital Products	**Component Assemblies**	**Service Contracts**
	1st Commission Rate	4%	2%	10%
	2nd Commission Rate	6%	3%	15%

Figure 5-30 Linked commission—product rates with hurdle.

Figure 5-31 Linked commission—with multiplier.

18. TI: Linked Commission—with Multiplier

Like other linked techniques, a multiplier requires two or more measures (see Figure 5-31). A multiplier provides greater pay discrimination than a hurdle. The payout impact of the multiplier varies given the performance range of the individual. A multiplier provides very clear direction on the importance of the first and second measure.

Figure 5-32 displays the payout schedule for a commission with a multiplier.

Component	Linked Commission With Multiplier		
Measure 1: Commission Rate		Performance To Goal	Commission Rate
	1st Commission Rate	To 100%	7%
	2nd Commission Rate	Above 100%	12%
Measure 2: Commission Multiplier	Performance to Goal on 2nd Measure	Multiplier of First Measure Earnings	
	Performance to Goal on 2nd Measure	Multiplier of Measure 1 Commission Earnings	
	120% and above	130%	
	110% to 119%	120%	
	105% to 109%	110%	
	100% to 104%	100%	
	95% to 99%	95%	
	90% to 94%	80%	
	80% to 89%	75%	
	Below 80%	50%	

Figure 5-32 Payout schedule for linked commission—with multiplier.

Observations

As Figure 5-32 illustrates, the payout impact is both positive (did exceed goal on the second measure) and negative (did not exceed goal on the second measure). Some organizations prefer to have only a positive multiplier with no negative deduction.

19. TI: Linked Commission—with Matrix

The final link design is a matrix (see Figure 5-33). Use a matrix when the company wants the salesperson to resolve two competing objectives. For example, (1) grow revenue but (2) sell profitably, or (1) retain existing customers but (2) add new customers, or (1) sell the core business but (2) sell new products, too. Anytime you wish the salesperson to reconcile competing objectives, a matrix is an excellent formula mechanic.

With a matrix, the salesperson—who in this case has pricing latitude—needs to sell over-target and with a high average gross margin to be eligible for commission rates greater than 5 percent. Exceptional performance on both measures (volume and average gross margin) can provide a commission rate as high as 9 percent for all sales revenue.

Percent of Sales Revenue Dollars/Month

Excellence	2.0	3.0	3.9	4.9	5.9	6.7	7.4	8.2	9.0
	1.8	2.8	3.7	4.7	5.7	6.3	7.0	7.7	8.3
	1.6	2.5	3.5	4.5	5.4	6.0	6.6	7.1	7.7
	1.3	2.3	3.3	4.3	5.2	5.7	6.1	6.6	7.0
Target	1.1	2.1	2.1	4.0	5.0	6.3	5.7	6.0	6.3
	0.8	1.7	2.5	3.3	4.2	4.5	4.8	5.2	5.5
	0.6	1.3	1.9	2.6	3.3	3.7	4.0	4.3	4.7
	0.3	0.8	1.4	1.9	2.5	2.8	3.2	3.5	3.8
Threshold	0.0	.04	.08	1.3	1.7	2.0	2.3	2.7	3.0

Sales Volume to Goal (vertical axis); Average Gross Margin to Goal (horizontal axis: Threshold, Target, Excellence)

Figure 5-33 TI-Linked commission—with matrix.

Note the following features of a matrix:

- The salesperson must resolve two conflicting measures—in this case, sales volume versus profits.
- There is a double threshold at the low end.
- Average gross margin has a higher importance weighting in the matrix than sales volume goal attainment. Average gross margin is weighted 60 percent, and sales volume goal attainment is weighted 40 percent in the matrix.
- Target "quota" can be the same for all salespeople, assuming territories are of equal size and opportunity, or can vary by salesperson.
- Matrices normally feature an odd number of rows and columns to provide a middle cell for presenting the target rate. Most matrices are at least 9×9 and some are as large as 15×15.

Observations

Matrices are ideally suited to provide rewards when there are two competing measures. Because of its visual display, salespeople readily understand how their performance impacts their pay.

Hurting Profits by Rewarding Profits. Senior management was perplexed to learn that the gross profit measure in the incentive plan actually hurt profits. Distribution companies sell what others manufacture. Multiline wholesalers purchase products from numerous manufacturers, bring them into inventory, and sell to the local market. The key measure of sales success is gross margin dollars—sales price less loaded cost of goods. Management correctly provided sales personnel with pricing flexibility to meet competitive pressures. To reward high sales with high pricing, management structured the incentive plan to pay a flat commission rate on all gross margin dollars. Unfortunately, it had the unintended consequence of reducing pricing. Why? Rather than keep prices high and risk losing the sale, sales personnel would reduce pricing to save the order. A commission on a few gross margin dollars is better than a commission on no gross margin dollars.

Preferred Solution. Create a payout schedule that pays a higher commission rate on gross margin dollars for orders with higher gross margin percent.

20. TI: Commission—for Stratified Sales Force

This final commission technique provides a method for rewarding sellers in a stratified sales organization.

A stratified sales force groups accounts by size and potential. Large accounts fall into Strategic Accounts; mid-size accounts belong to Major accounts; and small accounts are assigned to the General Business market.

Account stratification groups sales territories by size. From a sales compensation perspective, this configuration supports the use of commission plans. The groupings keep like-size territories together. Each job by category has its own commission rate correctly sized to the volume opportunity and target incentive opportunity for that category. Figure 5-34 shows that the larger territories have lower commission rates than the smaller territories.

Component	Commission Rates for Stratified Sales Force		
		Below Quota	Equal and Above Quota
Commission Rates	Global Account Executives	1.5%	2.0%
	Major Account Managers	3.0%	4.5%
	Territory Sales Representatives	6.0%	8.5%

Figure 5-34 Commission—for stratified sales force.

However, the volumes are much larger, assuring a higher payout for the larger territories, even though the effective commission rate is lower.

Observations

Stratification can provide the right type of payouts, but defending the lower commission rates for the larger accounts and territories will require continual explanation.

BONUS FORMULA: PROVIDING EQUAL EARNING OPPORTUNITIES WHEN TERRITORIES ARE DISSIMILAR IN SIZE

As noted earlier, commission formulas pay an established rate for sales production (for example, revenue, gross margins, or units sold). The commission schedule is constant for all sales personnel in the same position. Individual quotas may affect access to different ramp levels, but, for the most part, payments are similar for similar levels of sales production. Target incentive commission plans require territories to have similar sales potential. Sales organizations use account assignment and reassignment to keep territories balanced.

Organizations with the latitude to make account changes can easily keep earnings comparable by equalizing the sales-loading among sales personnel through account reassignments. This is not a preferred practice for income producers, but in the case of sales representatives, managing territory size through account assignments ensures that target incentive pay opportunities remain comparable among sales personnel. However, in some instances, it's not plausible to reassign accounts. In these cases, the movement of accounts is disruptive to customers and sales personnel. Simple geographic realities do not always allow for reassignment to other sales personnel to "balance" territories.

TARGET BONUS PLANS

As we have seen, commission pay plans provide an absolute rate for sales production. Bonus formula techniques, on the other hand, pay for relative performance against a percent of quota attainment. The bonus formula translates sales production into to a percent of quota accomplishment. The payout of the target incentive is a function of percent to goal achievement.

Figure 5-35 illustrates how a bonus formula equalizes earning opportunities.

A bonus formula allows sales management to pay for sales results as a percent of quota rather than a percent of actual sales production. There are numerous reasons for doing this, but the most compelling reason is that actual sales volume production does not always equate to sales accomplishment. For example, the size of large territories may be a function of account buying patterns rather than the persuasive selling skills of the salesperson.

A bonus formula requires the following:

- A target incentive earning amount, such as a flat dollar, percent of base salary, percent of total target compensation, or percent of a pool of monies
- A quota
- An incentive formula expressed as a portion of the target incentive amount for percent accomplishment of target quota

Bonus Formula Example

Territories	Sales Volume	Incentive Payment at 100% to Quota
Territory A	$4,500,000	$40,000
Territory B	$2,300,000	$40,000
Territory C	$9,300,000	$40,000

Figure 5-35 Bonus formula example.

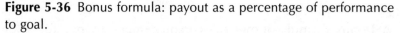

Figure 5-36 Bonus formula: payout as a percentage of performance to goal.

In all the examples that follow, and as depicted in Figure 5-36, sales production is expressed as a percent of 100 percent to quota and not actual dollar, margin, or unit sales.

Note that previous Plans 1 through 5 are Unit Rate plans and that Plans 6 through 20 are TI-Commission plans. In this section, we present the following sales representative TI-Bonus formulas (Plans 21–26):

21. Bonus—Individual Commission Rate
22. Bonus—Steps
23. Bonus—Formula Rate
24. Linked Bonus—Hurdle
25. Linked Bonus—Multiplier
26. Linked Bonus—Matrix

21. TI: Bonus—Individual Commission Rate

As territory size becomes more dissimilar, the use of commission programs becomes more problematic. The eventual solution is the use of a bonus formula method that pays a percent of target incentive as a percent of quota accomplishment. Prior

$$\frac{\text{Individual Target Incentive}}{\text{Individual Sales Quota}} \times 100 = \text{ICR}$$

For example:

Sales Representative A   ICR $\dfrac{\$60,000}{\$2,500,000} \times 100 = 2.40\%$

Sales Representative B   ICR $\dfrac{\$58,000}{\$1,900,000} \times 100 = 3.05\%$

Figure 5-37 How to calculate an individual commission rate.

to adopting a bonus formula, a commission-like arrangement provides different commission rates by salesperson/territory in order to equalize the earning opportunities of dissimilar-sized territories.

An individual commission rate (ICR) provides each person with his or her own commission rate. The purpose of ICRs is to manage payouts to a similar target incentive amount even though territories are dissimilar in size.

Sales management creates an ICR for each salesperson by dividing that person's target incentive amount (which may be unique for him or her) by the unique quota sales volume expected for the territory.

Figure 5-37 illustrates how to calculate ICR.

In this manner, sales management assigns an individual ICR to each salesperson.

Figure 5-38 is an incentive plan using an ICR.

Component	Individual Commission Rate (ICR) Schedule		
		Quota Performance	Commission Rate
Commission Rates	1st Commission Rate	0–100%	ICR%
	2nd Commission Rate	Over 100%	ICR% x 1.5

Figure 5-38 Sample individual commission rate (ICR) schedule.

ICR: A COMMISSION OR A BONUS?

An ICR has all the outward appearances of a commission. It pays for each sales occurrence. However, it accomplishes what a bonus formula does—equalizing the earning opportunity regardless of the size of territory.

Observations

ICR provides a transition formula technique between commission and bonus formulas. Most companies eventually adopt a bonus formula plan after several years with an ICR program.

22. TI: Bonus—Steps

The most common bonus application is the bonus step formula (see Figure 5-39). The bonus step formula provides higher earnings for higher percent performance to quota on a step basis.

This bonus step formula expressed as a percentage of base salary (see Figure 5-40) has a threshold and a cap. There is no interpretation between steps. Performance between steps pays the rate of the lower step.

Figure 5-39 Bonus step formula.

Component	Bonus Step Formula—Percent Times Base Salary	
Part 1: Base Salary	**Annual Base Salary** $80,000	
Part 2: Bonus Schedule	Bonus paid as a percent of base salary: **Sales Performance** **Percent to Goal**	**Bonus: %** **Base Salary**
	150% and over	105%
	125% to 149%	85%
	110% to 124%	65%
	105% to 109%	50%
	100% to 104%	35%
	90% to 99%	15%
	80% to 89%	5%
	Below 80%	0%

Figure 5-40 Bonus step formula—percent of base salary.

Figure 5-41 is the same structure but uses target incentive instead of base salary as the payout basis.

In both bonus step formulas just presented, the payout amounts are very similar. The only difference is the basis used for the target incentive—base salary is used in the first example, and target incentive is used in the second example. Both approaches are effective. One elevates the importance of the base salary, while the other

Component	Bonus Step Formula—Percent Times Target Incentive	
Part 1: Base Salary	**Annual Target Incentive** $22,750	
Part 2: Bonus Schedule	Bonus paid as a percent of base salary: **Sales Performance** **Percent to Goal**	**Bonus: %** **Target Incentive**
	150% and over	300%
	125% to 149%	245%
	110% to 124%	185%
	105% to 109%	142%
	100% to 104%	100%
	90% to 99%	45%
	80% to 89%	15%
	Below 80%	0%

Figure 5-41 Bonus step formula—percent of target incentive.

ignores the base salary and places significant emphasis on the target incentive amount. When using the target incentive amount, the dollars can be equal for all sales personnel in the same job or can vary based on sales management's value of the territory and contribution of the salesperson.

Observations

A bonus step formula is a means to equalize territories and provide varying payouts based on quota performance. The use of steps usually occurs when the performance range is wide and quota-setting confidence is moderate.

23. TI: Bonus—Formula Rate

Use a bonus formula rate (see Figures 5-42 and 5-43) to eliminate the cap and gaps in payout steps, which are both prominent features of the bonus step formula.

The bonus formula rate allows for payment over the full range of quota performance.

Figure 5-44 illustrates the payout for the formula presented in Figure 5-43 for three percentage levels of performance to quota: 50, 100, and 125.

Figure 5-42 Bonus—formula rate.

Component	Bonus Formula Rate	
Part 1: Target Incentive	**Annual Target Incentive** $45,000	
Part 2: Bonus Rate	Bonus paid as a percent of target incentive: **Bonus Payout Rate** Below Quota Each 1 percent of quota, 1% of target incentive At or Above Quota Each 1 percent of quota, 2% of target incentive	

Figure 5-43 Bonus formula rate—percentage of target incentive.

Observations

A bonus formula rate has the positive benefits of an uncapped plan similar to a commission program. However, it does require a two-step calculation to arrive at the incentive earning.

24. TI-Linked Bonus—Hurdle

Bonus plans can use the same linkage methods as commission plans, such as hurdles, multipliers, and matrices.

Bonus plans can use hurdles to tie two or more performance measures together. As illustrated in Figure 5-45, the retention rate of current customers acts as a hurdle affecting the bonus payout schedule.

Sample Bonus Payouts for Bonus Formula Rate

	Sales Result	Payout	Calculation
	50%	$12,500	50% x $25,000 = $12,500
or			
	100%	$25,000	100% x $25,000 = $25,000
or			
	125%	$37,500	(100% x $25,000) + (2% x 25 x $25,000) = $37,500

Figure 5-44 Payout examples for the bonus formula rate shown in Figure 5-43.

Component	Linked Bonus—Hurdle		
Part 1: Base Salary	**Salary Range/Year**		
	Minimum $56,000	**Midpoint** $70,000	**Maximum** $84,000
Part 2: Bonus Schedule	Bonus paid as a percent of midpoint: **Sales Performance** **Percent to Goal** 115% and over 110% to 114% 105% to 109% 100% to 104% 90% to 99% 80% to 89% Below 80% Hurdle: No incentive can be earned past 100% of goal unless the retention rate is greater than 80% of last year's sales revenue from existing customers.		**Bonus: % of** **Base Salary** 75% 55% 40% 25% 20% 15% 0

Figure 5-45 Linked bonus—hurdle.

Observations

The hurdle in Figure 5-45 imposes a significant punitive treatment for not surpassing 80 percent of revenue retention. The incentive plan pays no incentive beyond 100 percent to goal unless the retention measure surpasses 80 percent of last year's number. This formula assumes that loss of existing customers is a significant problem within the control of the salesperson.

25. TI: Linked Bonus—Multiplier

In Figure 5-46, a bonus rate formula gains a product mix multiplier to help reward cross-selling of products.

Observations

Using a product mix multiplier with both upside opportunity and downside risk notifies the salesperson that cross-selling or achieving product mix goals are very important.

26. TI: Linked Bonus—Matrix

A bonus matrix, like a commission matrix, features two competing objectives. In Figure 5-47, the two measures are sales volume and

Component	Linked Bonus—Multiplier		
Part 1: Target Incentive	**Annual Target Incentive** $25,000		
Part 2: Bonus Rate	Bonus paid as a percent of target incentive: 	**Bonus Payout Rate**	
	Below Quota	Each 1% of quota, 1% of target incentive	
	At or Above Quota	Each 1% of quota, 2% of target incentive	
Part 3: Multiplier	Product mix multiplier is applied to the Bonus Rate payout:		
	Number of Products Reaching Goal	**Product Mix Multiplier Times Bonus Payout**	
	5 of 5	120%	
	4 of 5	110%	
	3 of 5	100%	
	2 of 5	90%	
	1 of 5	75%	

Figure 5-46 Linked bonus—multiplier.

price realization. Price realization is a measure of how close to list price the salesperson sells the product. The use of this measure is appropriate when the salesperson has some degree of pricing authority.

Percent of Quarterly Target Incentive

80.0	98.3	116.7	135.0	153.3	190.0	226.7	263.3	300.0
66.7	85.0	103.3	121.7	140.0	169.6	199.2	228.8	258.3
53.3	71.7	90.0	108.3	126.7	149.2	171.7	194.2	216.7
40.0	58.3	76.7	95.0	113.3	128.8	144.2	159.6	175.0
26.7	45.0	63.3	81.7	100.0	108.3	116.7	125.0	133.3
20.0	34.8	49.6	64.4	79.2	87.5	95.8	104.2	112.5
13.3	24.6	35.8	47.1	58.3	66.7	75.0	83.3	91.7
6.7	14.4	22.1	29.8	37.5	45.8	54.2	62.5	70.8
0.0	4.2	8.3	12.5	16.7	25.0	33.3	41.7	50.0

Excellence (top row)
Sales Volume % to Target — Target 100%
Threshold (bottom row)

Threshold — Target—100% — Excellence

**Price Realization
% to Target**

Figure 5-47 Linked bonus—matrix.

Observations

In the bonus matrix illustrated in Figure 5-47, we see that sales volume has a higher incentive weighting than price realization. This design has a double threshold and a double cap at the top end. The salesperson cannot earn greater than 300 percent of his or her target incentive.

BONUS—CALCULATION BASIS

A bonus formula has both a quota and a target incentive. The formula can express the target incentive as a percent of base salary, as a percent of target incentive, or as a dollar amount.

Figure 5-48 presents an equivalent payout schedule demonstrating that a bonus formula can use any one of these payout bases in the formula.

Bonus Formula Basis			
Target Compensation	$140,000		
Pay Mix (%)	80/20		
Target Compensation	$28,000		
Quota Performance	**Payout Expressed As ...**		
	Percent of Base Pay	**Percent of Target Incentive**	**Flat Dollar Amount**
140.00%	75%	300.00%	$84,000
135.00%	69%	275.00%	$77,000
130.00%	63%	250.00%	$70,000
125.00%	56%	225.00%	$63,000
120.00%	50%	200.00%	$56,000
115.00%	44%	175.00%	$49,000
110.00%	38%	150.00%	$42,000
105.00%	31%	125.00%	$35,000
100.00%	25%	100.00%	$28,000
95.00%	23%	90.00%	$25,200
90.00%	20%	80.00%	$22,400
85.00%	18%	70.00%	$19,600
80.00%	15%	60.00%	$16,800
75.00%	13%	50.00%	$14,000
70.00%	10%	40.00%	$11,200

Figure 5-48 Bonus formula basis.

Consider the following factors when selecting the bonus basis:

- Select the percentage of the base salary if the base salaries provide an important and legitimate distinction among sales personnel.
- Select the percent of the target incentive when the base salaries are diverse and job content is alike among all incumbents.
- Select the flat dollar amount when the value of the incentive opportunity is likely to be the same for all.

SPECIAL DESIGNS

The following reflects special designs for unique selling situations (Plans 27–33). These designs provide practical "work-around" solutions for common problems.

Remember that previous Plans 1 through 5 are Unit Rate plans, Plans 6 through 20 are TI Commission plans, and Plans 21 through 26 are TI Bonus plans.

In this section, we will present the following solutions:

27. Hybrid—Bonus Flip to a Commission
28. Hybrid—Bonus with Drop-In Commission
29. Key Sales Objectives (KSO)
30. Team Incentive—Specialist Model
31. Team Incentive—Collaborative Model
32. Team Incentive—Opportunity Event Award
33. Add-On: Product Payment

27. Hybrid—Bonus Flip to a Commission

An interesting variation of the bonus formula is to provide a bonus formula up to quota, then provide a commission rate for all sales past quota. See Figure 5-49.

Component	Bonus Flip to a Commission		
Commission Rates		Quota Performance	Incentive Rate
	1st Payout Rate	0–100%	1% of Base for 1% of Quota
	2nd Payout Rate	Over 100%	3% on All Sales

Figure 5-49 Bonus flip to a commission.

Observations

This hybrid model helps to equalize dissimilar-sized territories up to quota performance. But once above quota, dissimilar-sized territories now pay out according to actual sales performance.

28. Hybrid—Bonus with Drop-In Commission

Sometimes sales management will need the use of a hybrid bonus and commission plan (see Figure 5-50). An example is the drop-in commission rate. This technique uses a bonus formula to reward quota performance, but provides a drop-in commission rate to recognize and reward larger sales territories.

Component	Bonus with Drop-in Commission Rate	
Part 1: Base Salary	**Base Salary/Year** **$75,000**	
Part 2: Bonus Schedule	Bonus paid as a percent of base salary:	
	Sales Performance Percent to Goal	**Bonus: % of Base Salary**
	150% and over	105%
	125% to 149%	85%
	110% to 124%	65%
	105% to 109%	50%
	100% to 104%	35%
	90% to 99%	15%
	80% to 89%	5%
	Below 80%	0
Part 3: Drop-in Commission Rate	Drop-in Commission Rate (per Net Sales Revenue)	
	Sales Volume Between **$2,000,000 and $5,000,000**	
	Drop-in Commission Rate	1.5%

Figure 5-50 Bonus with drop-in commission rate.

Observations

The reason this technique is called a *drop-in* is that it provides additional sales rewards for a defined range—in this case, starting at $2,000,000 and terminating at $5,000,000.

29. Key Sales Objectives

In some instances, sales management needs to create unique incentive objectives for individual sales personnel. The use of a management by objectives (MBO) component provides the flexibility to craft unique measures for each salesperson. Although MBOs have a long history in the corporate environment, the sales force has recently adapted the MBO concept for sales situations. Key sales objectives (KSOs) provide a handy framework for sales executives to develop incentive payouts tied to individual performance.

Here are some of the design considerations when creating a KSO program:

- Balance KSOs by not letting any single measure be worth more than 50 percent and not less than 10 percent.
- Limit KSO measures to five or fewer.
- Select measures that impact sales results and are quantitative.
- Provide KSO visibility through a database accessible by senior sales management.
- Require two levels of supervisor review before final KSOs are established and payouts are made.
- Require two levels of supervisor review for any modifications during the program period.
- Provide 3× capped leverage for sales result measures.
- Provide 2× capped leverage for sales progression measures.
- Provide 1× capped for compliance with sales required activities and sales actions.

| Elements | KSO Commitments and Scoring Worksheet | | | | | |
	#1	#2	#3	#4	#5	Total
Factor	New Customers	Prepackaged Solutions	Target Discount Rate	Cancelled Orders	Customer HQ Visits	
Commitment Objectives	7 over $500K in Sales	15 Signed Contracts	8%	<5%	5/Quarter	
Weighting	30%	25%	25%	15%	15%	
Point Value (A)	30	25	25	15	15	
Performance to Goal (B)	110%	120%	85%	75%	50%	
Performance Point Value A x B =	33	30	21.25	11.25	7.5	103
Performance Comments						
Authorization	Date:					

Figure 5-51 KSO commitments and scoring worksheet.

A preferred method is to use a point system to assign and calculate the KSO values and payout scores (see Figure 5-51). One approach uses a 200-point maximum scoring scheme with 100 being considered par, or expected performance. The KSO worksheet divides the target 100 points depending on the weighting of the KSO performance elements.

Figure 5-52 illustrates the conversion of points to bonus percentage payouts.

Component	KSO Point Payout Schedule	
Target Incentive	**KSO Target Incentive** $5,000	
KSO Payout Schedule	**Points**	**Percent of Target Incentive**
	175–200	150%
	150–174	125%
	125–149	110%
	105–124	105%
	95–104	100%
	75–94	75%
	50–74	25%
	Below 50	0%

Figure 5-52 KSO point payout schedule.

Observations

The target incentive amount can vary by salesperson. In this design, as is typical with KSO programs, the incentive payout is capped. Most KSOs are set quarterly, some annually.

30. Team Incentive—Specialist Model

Dedicated sales teams have members who are permanently assigned as specialists to the customer team. An account executive usually leads this team. Depending on the sales coverage model, the team may include the following personnel: additional sales representatives, technical presales support, contract management, fulfillment administration, installation personnel, and customer service.

The specialist model is the least team centric sales model. The leader of the sales unit, the account executive, orchestrates team efforts through the assignment of duties to team specialists. Each specialist contributes to the final sales results by performing his or her assigned duties. This type of team features a classic command-and-control model consistent with typical hierarchical work units. Figure 5-53 offers a possible incentive plan for this type of sales team.

Team Member Incentive Plans

Jobs	Incentive Elements	Weighting
Account Manager	Total Account Sales Volume*	60%
	Account Profitability	25%
	Individual KSOs	15%
Sales Representatives	Total Account Sales Volume*	45%
	Assigned Unit Sales Volume	40%
	Individual KSOs	15%
Pre-Sales Support	Total Account Sales Volume*	75%
	Individual KSOs	25%
Customer Service	Total Account Sales Volume*	75%
	Individual KSOs	25%

*Shared goal among all team specialists

Figure 5-53 Team incentive—specialist model.

In Figure 5-53, each team member shares at least one team measure: Total Account Sales. While each person has his or her own incentive plan, by sharing a common goal, the program provides support to a team goal.

Observations

This type of team incentive keeps team members focused on their assigned duties. The team members earn a portion of their incentive on the team's success and a portion on their personal accomplishments on behalf of the team. Since each team member has a unique incentive plan, the team incentive aspect of the plan derives from the shared "total account sales" measure that each team member has.

31. Team Incentive—Collaborative Model

The collaborative team model uses joint decision-making and shared work content to achieve a common account goal. These collaborative sales teams see team members as co-equals. The appropriate sales compensation program provides the same reward structure for all team members. Figure 5-54 is an example of a matrix incentive for collaborative teams.

Observations

All team members share in the same team award. This shared matrix approach supports a collaborative management approach. To achieve absolute egalitarianism, configure the matrix with actual dollars so that payouts are equal regardless of job assignment.

32. Team Incentive—Opportunity Event Award

Many sales teams are assembled to meet emerging customer-buying opportunities. These teams are not permanent, but temporarily

Component	Team Incentive—Collaborative Model		
Part 1: Base Salary Range		**Base Salary Range**	
		Minimum / Midpoint / Maximum	

Component	Team Incentive—Collaborative Model
Part 1: Base Salary Range	**Base Salary Range** **Account Manager** — Minimum $xx,xxx / Midpoint $xx,xxx / Maximum $xx,xxx **Sales Representatives** — $xx,xxx / $xx,xxx / $xx,xxx **Presales Support** — $xx,xxx / $xx,xxx / $xx,xxx **Customer Service** — $xx,xxx / $xx,xxx / $xx,xxx
Part 2: Annual Sales Team Award	**Annual Sales Team Award** **Percent of Base Salary Midpoint**

Sales Volume (Part 2)

3.0	3.9	4.8	5.6	6.5	7.4	8.3	9.1	10.0
2.6	3.5	4.4	5.3	6.1	6.9	7.6	8.4	9.1
2.3	3.1	4.0	4.9	5.8	6.4	7.0	7.6	8.3
1.9	2.8	3.6	4.5	5.4	5.9	6.4	6.9	7.4
1.5	2.4	3.3	4.1	5.0	5.4	5.8	6.1	6.5
0	0	0	0	4.1	4.5	4.9	5.3	5.6
0	0	0	0	3.3	3.6	4.0	4.4	4.8
0	0	0	0	2.4	2,8	3.1	3.5	3.9
0	0	0	0	1.5	1.9	2.3	2.6	3.0

Target
Performance

Figure 5-54 Team incentive—collaborative model.

configured to prepare a customer proposal and to present the company's complete value proposition. Normally, the specialists assigned to these teams participate in a gainsharing plan or other corporate team program, or simply are paid a base salary with annual merit adjustments. Select companies, however, like to provide an award to these individuals for assisting with a sales effort. Often, these pay plans are add-on spot awards.

A common payout method for opportunity teams is an event award paid at the time of a significant event such as a contract signing as shown in Figure 5-55.

Observations

These nominal rewards provide recognition for sales support during the sales process. The account executive and sales personnel would be on a normal sales compensation program.

Paid at Contract Acceptance

	Contract Value		
	$2M–$4.9M	$5M–15M	>$15M
Presales Support Specialist	$100	$150	$250
Contracts Specialist	$ 75	$125	$175
Service Coordinator	$ 75	$125	$175
Installation Specialist	$ 50	$ 75	$100

Figure 5-55 Team incentive—opportunity event award.

Add-On Plans

Add-on plans have no reduction in base salaries. Such plans provide an upside earning opportunity over expected performance. If correctly designed, the plan provides no payments for below-target performance.

33. Add-On: Product Payment

For some customer service jobs, there may be an opportunity to do additional sales to customers. For example, bank tellers might have the opportunity to refer customers to sales specialists. An add-on bonus, above a competitive base salary, would provide additional earnings for any fulfilled referral. Figure 5-56 provides an example of a product payout schedule.

Observations

Add-on product payment plans provide additional earnings for additional effort over the normal expectations for a job. However, not all employees embrace such plans. The outcome produces uneven performance by employees with only a low percentage (below 20 percent) performing well.

BASE SALARIES

Base salaries for sales representatives can represent a substantial portion of compensation earnings. The following

Product Payments
(Closed Business)

Product	Dollar Amt
Private Banking	$55.00
Securities	$50.00
Line of Credit	$25.00
Auto Loan	$15.00
Credit Card	$ 5.00
Overdraft	$ 5.00
Internet Offer	$ 2.50

Figure 5-56 Add-on—product payment.

methods are available to manage base salary. These base salary methods apply whether the job has an incentive opportunity or not.

Remember that previous Plans 1 through 5 are Unit Rate plans, Plans 6 through 20 are TI Commission plans, Plans 21 through 26 are TI Bonus plans, Plans 27 through 32 are Special Designs, and Plan 33 is an Add-On plan. We will now describe four methods to manage base salaries (Plans 34–37):

34. Fixed Dollar—Job Rates
35. Fixed Dollar—Quota Levels
36. Base Salary Range
37. Total Compensation Range

34. Base Salary: Fixed Dollar—Job Rates

When base salaries are low, sales management can assign a fixed dollar per job title. All incumbents receive the same base salary level. Promotion to higher level jobs allows for an increase in base salary levels. While the job content of each higher level job might be similar to the current job, the promotion rewards sustained

Component	Different Sales Jobs	
Salary Levels by Job	**Jobs**	**Base Pay**
	Job A	$75,000
	Job B	$70,000
	Job C	$65,000
	Job D	$50,000
	Job E	$40,000

Figure 5-57 Base salary-fixed dollar—job rates.

contribution, sales effectiveness, and other measures such as cumulative sales or certification levels.

The base salary schedule in Figure 5-57 provides an increasing level of base pay tied to job title. These pay levels might be reviewed and increased each year.

Observations

Fixed job rates provide good motivation to focus on getting promoted. Management can use promotion criteria to reward long-term results or other types of nonsales measures.

35. Base Salary: Fixed Dollar—Quota Levels

A base salary fixed dollar—quota levels plan, provides higher levels of base salary for those who sustain higher sales levels. In the simplest model, as illustrated in Figure 5-58, the base salary for the new year is established by sales performance in the previous year.

	Base Salary Fixed Dollar—Quota Levels	
Component Salary Steps	**Last Year** **Sales Performance**	**This Year** **Base Salary Amount**
	Below $1M	$65,000
	$1M–$2.9M	$70,000
	$3M–$5M	$95,000
	Over $5M	$110,000

Figure 5-58 Base salary-fixed dollar—quota levels.

Observations

Varying the base salary depending on the previous year's perform-ance provides a good reward to excel. Unfortunately, for these models to work effectively, sales management must reduce base pay if the level of sales performance drops into a lower category. This event will most likely trigger significant terminations.

36. Base Salary Range

Often companies provide a separate pay range structure for sales positions. When base salaries represent 65 percent of total target cash compensation, the base salary is large enough to participate in the annual merit increase program. However, because the pay mixes differ by sales job, the HR/compensation manager needs to create job-specific salary ranges.

Figure 5-59 illustrates a sample salary range structure. On an annual basis, the merit increase program provides suggested pay guidelines depending on two factors: position in the grade of the existing base salary and performance rating.

Component	Base Salary Range						
Base Salary Range	Grades				Sales Salary Range		
	Grade	T-Comp	Title	Pay Mix	Min	Mid	Max
		65,000	Tele Rep	60/40	31,200	39,000	46,800
	E85	65,000	Sales Support	80/20	41,600	52,000	62,400
		65,000	Field Market	85/15	44,200	55,250	66,300
		95,000	Territory Rep	60/40	45,600	57,000	68,400
	E86	95,000	Channel Rep	70/30	53,200	66,500	79,800
		95,000	Named Accounts	80/20	60,800	76,000	91,200
		120,000	Major Account	75/25	67,500	90,000	101,250
	E87	120,000	National Account	80/20	76,800	96,000	115,200

Figure 5-59 Base salary range.

Component	Base Salary Total Compensation Range					
Target Total Compensation	Job: Senior Account Manager Total Compensation Range: $88,000—$120,000—$132,000 Pay Mix of Job: 70/30					
	Employee	T-Comp	T-Comp Increase	New T-Comp	Base	Target Incentive
Total Compensation Range	A. Jones	96,000	5%	$100,800	$70,560	$30,240
	R. Flangton	89,000	3%	$ 91,670	$64,169	$27,501
	B. Lister	126,000	2%	$128,520	$89,964	$38,556
	H. Pago	105,500	5%	$110,775	$77,543	$33,232

Figure 5-60 Base salary—total compensation range.

Observations

Base salary ranges are the most common method to manage base pay. However, most sales personnel will focus on the sales incentive component where they feel they can affect the most upside influence on their earnings.

37. Base Salary: Total Compensation Range

Some companies provide the annual increase on the total compensation for the salesperson. Sales management uses merit guidelines to determine the increase. Employees are told their new total compensation. Based on the pay mix for the job, the new total compensation number is then divided into two components: the base salary and the target incentive. Figure 5-60 presents an example of a total compensation range.

Observations

This approach ensures that the pay mix of the job remains constant. All incumbents will have the same ratio of base to incentive.

SUMMARY

While the list of incentive formulas in this chapter seems exten-sive and complete, it actually only represents the building blocks of incentive formula design. The combination of these different components gives the full palette of choices. The number of con-figurations is almost unlimited. However, limiting the number of performance measures to three or fewer precludes the occurrence of overly complex designs.

Chapter 6

Formula Construction

Sales compensation formula construction is all about mathematics. Fortunately, it's not very complex and is easily mastered. First, we will examine the fundamentals of constructing sales compensation formulas. Then, we will examine the economics of sales compensation for income producers. Finally, we will examine how to build target incentive commission and bonus formulas for sales representatives.

FUNDAMENTALS OF SALES COMPENSATION FORMULAS

$$\frac{\text{compensation}}{\text{performance}} = \text{payout rate}$$

The payout rate is calculated by dividing the compensation amount by the performance amount.

Using our payout graph (see Figure 6-1), we see the target compensation is $100,000 and the expected performance is $2,000,000.

The formula to calculate the payout rate (also known as the *slope* in the math world) is to simply divide the pay by the performance, or A divided by B, presented as a calculation:

$$\frac{\text{A compensation}}{\text{B performance}} = \text{payout rate (slope)}$$

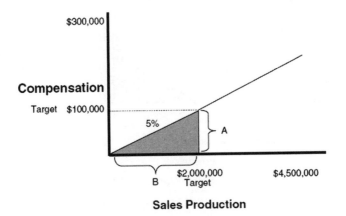

Figure 6-1 Flat commission—formula graph.

Here is the formula expressed as numbers:

$$\frac{\$100,000}{\$2,000,000} \times 100 = 5\%$$

Multiply by 100 to move the decimal point to change the resulting division outcome from .05 to 5% for notation purposes.

The flat commission schedule (see Figure 6-2) displays the sales compensation plan when published for sales personnel.

As illustrated in Figure 6-3, to calculate a second (progressive or regressive) payout rate, simply replicate the same calculation for the new upside pay opportunity and expected upside performance range.

The second payout rate is calculated using the same formula model. Because the first payout rate of 5% paid $100,000 for the

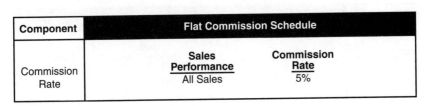

Figure 6-2 Flat commission schedule.

Figure 6-3 Straight commission second rate—formula graph.

first performance range of $2,000,000, eliminate these numbers from the equation when calculating the second payout rate.

$$\frac{C \text{ compensation}}{D \text{ performance}} = \text{payout rate}$$

Or the actual numbers:

$$\frac{\$300,000 - \$100,000}{\$4,500,000 - \$2,000,000} \times 100 = 8\%$$

The subtractions of $100,000 of target pay and $2,000,000 for target performance leaves the following division of upside compensation divided by upside performance:

$$\frac{\$200,000}{\$2,500,000} \times 100 = 8\%$$

The incentive plan pays 5 cents for every dollar of sales up to and including $2,000,000 and 8 cents for every dollar over $2,000,000 in sales. Figure 6-4 displays this commission schedule.

Component	Progressive Ramp Commission Schedule		
		Sales Performance	Commission Rate
Commission Rate	1st Commission Rate	To $2M	5%
	2nd Commission Rate	Over $2M	8%

Figure 6-4 Progressive ramp commission schedule.

For sales efforts that achieve $2,000,000 in sales, the payout is $100,000. For those sellers who close $4,500,000 in business, the sales compensation program will pay $300,000.

We will use this same fundamental formula calculation method when we construct compensation formulas for income producers and sales representatives including both TI-Commission and TI-Bonus formulas.

THE ECONOMICS OF INCOME PRODUCERS

The sales compensation plans for income producers should be simple: a fixed commission rate (flat) for all sales revenue. In some industries, the commission rate for income producers is so well established that few in sales management would even presume to question the rate, let alone alter it. Senior management simply accepts the rate for the income producers as a known constant built right into business planning assumptions of the company's financial model. However, like any economic statement, market forces have an ongoing influence on the development and refinement of income producer commission rates. No one should assume that commission rates are constant and cannot be changed.

As we examined earlier, income producers are independent sellers who have access to customers. The economic value of income producers is their ability to reach and influence buyers. Companies pay for this access by paying a commission for sales results. Most income producers' pay plans feature a flat (unchanging) commission rate. It's not unusual for the income producer to be a nonpayroll employee paid as a contract worker or separate business entity. Regardless of the legal relationship, there is a rational basis for setting and evaluating the commission rates paid to income producers.

Income producer commission rates vary by industry. While this is not an exact science, the trend is clear. Industries with high volumes per income producer tend to have lower commission rates, and

Figure 6-5 Commission rates for income producers vary by sales volume.

industries with lower volumes per producer tend to have higher commission rates. Management should constantly examine the expected volumes to determine if the commission rates are still effective, too high, or too low. In Figure 6-5 we see that commission rates differ by industry depending on the expected volume per income producer.

For one type of income producer—the independent manufacturer representative—the loss of the product line is a major, ongoing concern. A company has the option of replacing the independent reps with an in-house dedicated sales force. When this occurs, this is known as "taking the line direct." At a certain point, it may make more economic sense to terminate the independent reps and hire a company sales force. As shown in Figure 6-6, a financial analysis of the "switching point" will identify when it's better to use one sales coverage model versus another.

Figure 6-6 Cost of sales for income producers versus direct sales force.

As the overall volume of the line increases, it becomes more economically feasible to hire a direct sales force, particularly for large, ongoing purchases. This, of course, assumes that the direct sales force can establish buyer relationships and successfully displace the independent (income producer) reps. To calculate the switching point correctly, include both direct and indirect costs. Don't forget to add loss of sales during the changeover as a cost factor, too.

For some industries, historic commission rates seem to remain constant. In parts of the United States, the commission rate for residential real estate is 6 percent of the house sale price. The actual commission rate paid to the agent who sells your house is 1.5 percent. Three percent is assigned to the listing broker and 3 percent is assigned to the selling broker. The listing broker and the agent split the 3 percent, so the agent's actual commission rate is 1.5 percent of the sales price.

Certain electronic component segments pay a flat 10 percent to the manufacturer reps for all sales. Mass reach apparel can pay as low as 2 percent, whereas specialty apparel can pay as high as 15 percent. However, practices do vary from these norms and what the market will bear allows for a give and take in actual commission rates.

Most industries that maintain a constant income producer commission rate exhibit one of two traits: Either the market segment is very stable (food brokers) or employment levels vary greatly with market swings such as in real estate and stock brokerage.

ADVANCED THINKING ABOUT INCOME PRODUCER COMMISSION RATES

We suggest that companies consider the following adjustments to the traditional flat commission formula for income producers when presented with the following conditions:

- *Increase commission rates if the income producer is instrumental in adding substantial incremental growth.* Reward the economic

Component	Progressive Ramp Participation Rate			
Participation Rate	Commission Rate to Agency Varies by Product, Between 5% and 10%.			
		Seller Performance	Commission Split	
			Seller	Agency
	1st Participation Rate	To $5M	20%	80%
	2nd Participation Rate	$5M–$7.5M	22%	78%
	3rd Participation Rate	Over $7.5M	25%	75%

Figure 6-7 Progressive ramp participation rate.

contribution of the income producers when they singularly drive new revenue growth. Provide a progressive commission rate for these new dollars. A progressive ramp commission schedule motivates additional sales, recognizes contribution, and helps contribute to seller loyalty.

Figure 6-7 is an illustration of a progressive participation rate for an income producer. The agency (employer) gets a commission for selling a product line, in this case, 5 to 10 percent of the sale price. The principal of the agency then in turn splits this with the sellers who work for the agency. This split is known as the "participation rate."

Figure 6-8 is the method used to calculate the participation rate.

Progressive Ramp Participation Rate

Figure 6-8 Progressive ramp rate—calculation participation rate.

Participation Rate Schedule			
Agency Commissions	Avg. Agency Commission 7.5% of Actual Revenue	Target Payment to Income Producer	Percent Participation Rate
$ 5,000,000	$375,000	$ 75,000	20%
$ 7,500,000	$562,500	$116,250	22%
$10,000,000	$750,000	$163,125	25%

Figure 6-9 Participation rate schedule.

Figure 6-9 displays the participation schedule for the income producer—salesperson. The *Percent Participation Rate* is that share of the agency's commission given to the salesperson.

The first participation rate is calculated as follows:

$$\frac{\$75,000}{\$375,000} \times 100 = 20\%$$

The second participation rate is calculated as follows:

$$\frac{\$116,250 - \$75,000}{\$562,500 - \$375,000} \times 100 = 22\%$$

The third participation rate is calculated as follows:

$$\frac{\$163,125 - \$116,250}{\$750,000 - \$562,000} \times 100 = 25\%$$

Increasing the participation rate from 20 to 22 to 25 percent recognizance, in this case, is the pivotal role of the salesperson in securing additional business.

- *Decrease commission rates as volume increases when income producer is incidental to added growth:* While a regressive commission rate schedule may be motivationally challenging, in situations where additional sales volume (bluebirds) is not caused by exceptional sales efforts, then using regressive commission rates is appropriate.

- *Reduce sales compensation credits for recurring revenue:* Review crediting practices for recurring revenue. If the income producer is instrumental in maintaining and reselling the recurring revenue, then include all recurring revenue in incentive calculations. If recurring revenue is inherent in the original sale and does not require hands-on attention by the salesperson, reduce or discount recurring revenue. Consider terminating, after a period of time, the revenue credit on recurring revenue if the income producer's influence is inconsequential.
- *Establish a tiered producer program:* A tiered program provides different categories of commission participation depending on levels of performance, investment, certification, and exclusivity, for example, Platinum, Gold, and Silver, or I, II, and III. Tiered programs allow differentiated commission treatment.

Unlimited earnings—means just that: unlimited. The president of a privately held investment company was dismayed to learn that the top salesperson was to earn incentive payments five times what was expected. What was he to do? After years of lackluster performance, a new management team was brought in to revitalize the commercial real estate unit. With an uncapped incentive plan, the new team produced sales results in excess of any conceivable level. Now, faced with making payments far in excess of intended levels, what should the president do?

Preferred Solution: First, pay the incentive owed. A good lawyer will have no trouble in convincing a judge that the company is in breach of contract if it fails to pay. Second, redo the compensation plan to manage upside earnings. For example, use a regressive commission rate above a high sales level, or cap the earnings on any one order or account.

CONSTRUCTING SALES REPRESENTATIVE FORMULA

We use the same basic mathematical formula to construct a compensation formula for sales representatives that we use for income producers.

$$\frac{\text{compensation}}{\text{performance}} = \text{payout rate}$$

Again, compensation (the target payout amount) is divided by the performance (the preferred performance to earn the target compensation) to determine payout rate—whether a commission or bonus formula.

Follow these 10 steps to construct any sales representative sales compensation formula:

- *Step 1. Identify target total cash compensation (TTCC):* Begin by identifying the target total cash compensation for the job. This amount equals the preferred earnings levels (base plus incentive payment) for achieving expected results. This amount varies from one company to another. Some organizations follow labor market practices very closely, while others rely on internal equity. Often the amount reflects a balance of competing objectives: market rates, internal equity, cost, future objectives, and past practices. While TTCC represents a single number for a job, the actual target pay levels for specific individuals will most likely vary due to differences in base salary, or even a pay range allowing for variance in the target incentive amount.
- *Step 2. Determine the pay mix of the plan:* The pay mix is the split of the target total cash compensation into two components, a base salary and a target incentive amount. The more prominent (influential) the salesperson in the buying decision of the customer, the lower the base salary. The mix is expressed as a split of 100 percent (for example, 60/40, 70/30).

- *Step 3. Establish the pay leverage of the plan:* The leverage of the plan provides the target upside outstanding earning amount for achieving exceptional sales. The leverage is expressed as a multiplier of the target incentive. The most common leverage is "3×." That is, three times the target incentive (added back to the base salary) defines the outstanding pay level for excellent performance.

- *Step 4. Calculate range of pay opportunities:* The pay opportunities reflect the application of the company's target total cash compensation, mix, and leverage. Figure 6-10 illustrates that a TTCC of $100,000 with a mix of 50/50 and a leverage of 3× would provide the following pay opportunities:

Minimum pay (base salary)	$ 50,000
Target total cash compensation	$100,000
Outstanding pay	$200,000

$$(\$100{,}000 \times 0.5 \times 3) + \$50{,}000 = \$200{,}000$$

- *Step 5. Identify and weigh performance measures:* Performance measures give meaning to the sales compensation program. Performance measures are unique to the company and the job. The right performance measures will support a company's current sales objectives. Select three or fewer performance measures for

Figure 6-10 Range of pay opportunities.

	Target Dollars	Performance Measures and Weights		
		Sales Volume (50%)	Profits (25%)	Product Mix (25%)
Minimum Incentive Pay	$ 0	$ 0	$ 0	$ 0
Target Incentive Pay	$ 50,000	$25,000	$12,500	$12,500
Outstanding Incentive Pay	$100,000	$50,000	$50,500	$50,500
Over Base Total Outstanding	$150,000	$75,000	$37,500	$37,500

Figure 6-11 Performance measures and weights.

the sales compensation plan. Weigh the performance measures depending on their respective importance (see Figure 6-11). Allocate target ($50,000) and outstanding incentive dollars ($100,000), depending on these weightings.

- *Step 6. Confirm quota difficulty distribution:* Make sure that quota difficulty achieves a quota distribution of a predefined percent of the sales personnel who will perform at or better than quota performance, and a percent that will perform below quota (see Figure 6-12).

- *Step 7. Set performance expectations:* Set performance expectations for each performance measure: threshold, target, and excellence

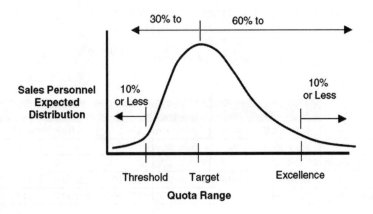

Figure 6-12 Quota distribution.

134 · COMPENSATING THE SALES FORCE

	Performance Expectations		
Performance	Sales Volume	Profits	New Products
Threshold	$1,750,000	$ 500,000	$250,000
Target	$3,000,000	$1,000,000	$500,000
Excellence	$4,500,000	$1,500,000	$750,000

Figure 6-13 Performance expectations.

(see Figure 6-13). The summation of the performance expectations for all sales jobs should equal the business forecast.

- *Step 8. Assign pay expectations with performance expectations:* Each performance level is assigned a payout amount (see Figure 6-14).
- *Step 9. Calculate the incentive formula for each performance measure:* The incentive formula for each measure can now be calculated. Again, we use the simple formula:

$$\frac{\text{compensation}}{\text{performance}} = \text{payout rate}$$

Sales Volume Commission Rates

First commission rate: threshold to target.

$$\frac{\$25,000}{\$3,000,000 - \$1,750,000} \times 100 = 2\%$$

Second commission rate: target to excellence.

$$\frac{\$50,000}{\$4,000,000 - \$3,000,000} \times 100 = 5\%$$

	Pay and Performance Expectations					
	Sales Volume		Profits		New Products	
	Volume	Pay	Volume	Pay	Volume	Pay
Minimum	$1,750,000	$ 0	$ 500,000	$ 0	$250,000	$ 0
Target	$3,000,000	$25,000	$1,000,000	$12,500	$500,000	$12,500
Outstanding	$4,000,000	$50,000	$1,500,000	$25,500	$750,000	$25,000

Figure 6-14 Pay and performance amounts.

Profit Commission Rates

First commission rate: threshold to target.

$$\frac{\$12,500}{\$1,000,000 - \$500,000} \times 100 = 2.5\%$$

Second commission rate: target to excellence.

$$\frac{\$25,000}{\$1,500,000 - \$1,000,000} \times 100 = 5.0\%$$

New Product Commission Rates

First commission rate.

$$\frac{\$12,500}{\$500,000 - \$250,000} \times 100 = 5\%$$

Second commission rate.

$$\frac{\$50,000}{\$750,000 - \$500,000} \times 100 = 10\%$$

- *Step 10. Publish incentive formula:* Now the incentive formula can be published for the sales personnel (see Figure 6-15).

Component	Commission Program—3 Measures		
Base Salary	$0–(Straight Commission)		
Sales Volume Commission Rate		**Sales Production**	**Commission Rate**
	To Threshold	0–$1,750,000	0%
	Threshold to Target	$1,750,001–$3,000,000	2%
	Over Target	Over $3,000,000	5%
Profit Commission Rate		**Profit Production**	**Commission Rate**
	To Threshold	0–$500,000	0%
	Threshold to Target	$500,001–$1,000,000	2.5%
	Over Target	Over $1,000,000	5%
New Product Commission Rate		**New Sales Production**	**Commission Rate**
	To Threshold	0–$250,000	0%
	Threshold to Target	$250,001–$500,000	2%
	Over Target	Over $500,000	5%

Figure 6-15 Commission program.

FORMULA CONSTRUCTION WORKSHEETS

The following worksheets present a uniform method for construct-ing a compensation formula. These worksheets are the most popular sales compensation formulas:

1. Progressive ramp commission with base salary
2. Commission program with a multiplier and base salary
3. Bonus formula with steps
4. Bonus formula rate
5. Bonus formula matrix

Worksheet 1: Progressive Ramp Commission with Base Salary

This sales compensation formula pays commission on all sales (see Figures. 6-16 and 6-17). The commission rate has a progressive ramp and is uncapped. There is no threshold. Performance is 100 percent of sales volume. The plan provides a single base salary level for all job incumbents.

	Steps	Formula Parameters	
1	Total Target Compensation	$95,000	
2	Pay Mix	70/30	
3	Leverage	3×	
4	Pay Opportunities	Base Salary:	$66,500 ($95,000 × .70 = $66,500)
		Target Incentive:	$28,500 ($95,000 × .30 = $28,500)
		Outstanding Pay:	$152,000 ($28,500 × 3 + $66,500 = $152,000)
5	Measures and Weights	Sales Volume:	100%
6	Quota Distribution	Meet/Exceed Target:	60%−70%
		Below Target:	30%−40%
7	Performance Expectations	Threshold:	$0
		Target Performance:	$1,000,000
		Excellence:	$2,000,000

8	Assign Pay Opportunities to Performance Expectations		**Performance Levels**	**Pay Opportunities**
		Threshold:	$ 0	$66,500 (Base Salary)
		Target:	$1,000,000	$28,500 (Target Pay)
		Excellence:	$2,000,000	$57,000 (Outstanding Pay)
9	Calculate Formula	1st Commission Rate $$\frac{28,500}{1,000,000} \times 100 = 2.85\%$$ 2nd Commission Rate $$\frac{\$152,000 - 95,000}{2,000,000 - 1,000,000} \times 100 = 5.7\%$$		
10	Publish Formula	**Sales Volume Production**	**Commission Rate**	
		0–1,000,000	2.85%	
		Over 1,000,000	5.70%	

Figure 6-16 Worksheet 1—progressive ramp commission with base salary.

Worksheet 2: Commission Program with a Multiplier and Base Salary

This sales compensation plan has a base salary range and a commission on all sales, with no threshold (see Figure 6-18). There are two measures: sales volume and gross margin. Gross margin is a linked multiplier measure that increases or decreases the value of the sales volume commission based on gross margin performance. Sales volume is weighted 70 percent in the plan; gross margin is weighted 30 percent.

Figure 6-17 Progressive ramp commission with base salary.

	Steps	Formula Parameters
1	Total Target Compensation	$60,000
2	Pay Mix	75/25
3	Leverage	3×
4	Pay Opportunities	**Base Salary Range** Minimum: $36,000 ($45,000 × .80 = $36,000) Midpoint: $45,000 ($60,000 × .75 = $45,000) Maximum: $54,000 ($45,000 × 1.2 = $54,000) Target Base Salary: $45,000 (75% of $60,000) Target Incentive: $15,000 (25% of $60,000) Outstanding Pay: $90,000 (15,000 × 3 + $45,000) = $90,000
5	Measures and Weights	Sales Volume: 70% $10,500 ($15,000 × .70) = $10,500 Gross Margin Percent: 30% $ 4,500 ($15,000 × .30) = $ 4,500
6	Quota Distribution	Meet/Exceed Target: 60%–70% Below Target: 30%–40%

7 Performance Expectations

Performance Range

	Revenue	Gross Margin Percent
Threshold:	$ 0	23%
Target Performance:	$ 750,000	26%
Excellence Performance:	$1,500,000	31%

8 Assign Pay Opportunities to Performance Expectations

Total Pay Opportunity

	Components	Cumulative
Threshold:	$45,000 (Base Salary)	$45,000
Target Incentive:	$15,000	$60,000
Excellence:	$30,000 (Outstanding Pay)	$90,000

Pay Components by Performance Measure

	Sales Volume		Gross Margin	
	Result	Pay	Result	Multiple
Threshold:	$ 0	$ 0	23%	($ 4,500)*
Target:	$ 750,000	$15,000	26%	$ 0
Excellence:	$1,500,000	$30,000	31%	$15,000

*$4,500 is potential monies at risk for performing between 23% and 26% gross margin. Amount to be deducted from sales volume commission dollars.

9 Calculate Formula

Sales Volume Commission Rates

1st Commission Rate

$$\frac{15,000}{\$750,000} \times 100 = 2.0\%$$

2nd Commission Rate

$$\frac{\$30,000 - 15,000}{1,500,000 - 750,000} \times 100 = 2.0\%$$

thus,

$$\frac{\$15,000}{\$750,000} \times 100 = 2.0\%$$

		The first and second commission rates are the same. This provides a 2× payout. To earn the 3× payout, the sales representative must excel on the profit multiplier.

Profit Multiplier

To calculate the multiplier, determine the percent available for each percent of gross margin achieved:

The **take-away** multiplier for below-target performance:
$$\frac{(\$4,500)/\$15,000}{26-23} = (.10)$$

The **additive** multiplier rate for each percent of gross margin performance for above target performance:
$$\frac{(\$45,000-\$30,000)/\$30,000}{31-26} = .10$$

The schedule for the multiplier is as follows:

Gross Margin	Rate	Multiplier of Commission Dollars
23%	(.10)	70%
24%	(.10)	80%
25%	(.10)	90%
26%	0%	100%
27%	.10	110%
28%	.10	120%
29%	.10	130%
30%	.10	140%
31%	.10	150%

10 Publish Formula

Base Salary Range

Minimum	Midpoint	Maximum
$36,000	$45,000	$54,000

Sales Volume Commission Formula

Sales Volume Production	Commission Rate
All Sales	2%

Gross Margin Multiplier (Percent of Commission Dollars)

Gross Margin	Multiplier
23%	70%
24%	80%
25%	90%
26%	100%
27%	110%
28%	120%
29%	130%
30%	140%
31%	150%

Figure 6-18 Worksheet 2—commission program with profit multiplier and base salary.

Worksheet 3: Bonus Formula with Steps

Worksheet 3 (Figure 6-19) shows how to calculate a bonus formula with steps, a base salary, and a performance threshold.

	Steps	Formula Parameters		
1	Total Target Compensation	$100,000		
2	Pay Mix	75/25		
3	Leverage	3×		

4	Pay Opportunities	Base Salary Range
		  Minimum: $60,000 ($75,000 × .8 = $60,000)
		  Midpoint: $75,000 ($100,000 × .75 = $75,000)
		  Maximum: $90,000 ($75,000 × 1.2 = $90,000)
		Target Base Salary: $75,000 ($100,000 × .75 = $75,000)
		Target Incentive: $25,000 ($100,000 × .25 = $25,000)
		Outstanding Pay: $150,000 ($25,000 × 3 = $75,000 = $150,000)		

5	Measures and Weights	Sales Volume: 100%		
6	Quota Distribution	Meet/Exceed Target: 60%−70% Below Target: 30%−40%		

7	Performance Expectations	**Performance Range**
		                               Revenue
		                          Percent to Goal
		Threshold: 50%
		Target Performance: 100%
		Excellence Performance: 140%		

8	Assign Pay Opportunities to Performance Expectations	**Total Pay Opportunity**
		
		                    Components Cumulative
		Threshold: $75,000 (base salary) $ 75,000
		Target Incentive: $25,000 $100,000
		Excellence: $50,000 (Outstanding Pay) $150,000
		<hr>**Pay Compensation By Performance Measure**
		                       Sales Volume
		                  Result* Pay
		Minimum: 60% $ 5,000
		Target: 100% $25,000
		Outstanding: 140% $50,000
		*Sales results are expressed as a percent of quota performance		

9	Calculate Formula	**Bonus Formula Payout Steps** Calculate payout in four steps of 10% increments. Express payout as a percent of target incentive ($25,000)		

To calculate the bonus formula steps, determine the value of each step for below quota performance and then for above quota performance.

<u>Below quota performance:</u> Calculate the steps for below target performance:

$$\frac{(\$25,000)/\$25,000}{(100-50)/10} = .20$$

<u>Above quota performance:</u> Calculate the steps for above target performance.

$$\frac{\$50,000/\$25,000}{(140-100)/10} = .50$$

The schedule for the steps is as follows:

Percent Quota	Rate	Percent of Target Incentive
50%	.00	0%
60%	.20	20%
70%	.20	40%
80%	.20	60%
90%	.20	80%
100%	.20	100%
110%	.50	150%
120%	.50	200%
130%	.50	250%
140%	.50	300%

10 | **Publish Formula**

Base Salary Range

Minimum	Midpoint	Maximum
$60,000	$75,000	$90,000

Bonus Steps
Paid as a percent of target incentive

Percent to Quota	Percent of Target Incentive
50%	0%
60%	20%
70%	40%
80%	60%
90%	80%
100%	100%
110%	150%
120%	200%
130%	250%
140%	300%

Figure 6-19 Worksheet 3—bonus formula with steps.

Worksheet 4: Bonus Formula Rate

This bonus formula rate (see Figures 6-20 and 6-21) provides payouts for each percent of quota performance. The plan has a base salary and a performance threshold. Bonus rate is expressed as a percent of salary range midpoint. Use bonus formula rate when performance range is narrow and each percent of quota is significant. As a bonus formula, dissimilar-sized territories are "made equal" for compensation purposes by tying payouts to percent of quota performance, regardless of actual quota volume.

	Steps	Formula Parameters		
1	Total Target Compensation	$80,000		
2	Pay Mix	80/20		
3	Leverage	3×		
4	Pay Opportunities	**Base Salary Range**		
		Minimum:	$51,200 ($64,000 × .8 = $51,200)	
		Midpoint:	$64,000 ($80,000 × .8 = $64,000)	
		Maximum:	$78,000 ($64,000 × 1.2 = $78,000)	
		Target Base Salary:	$64,000 ($80,000 × .80 = $64,000)	
		Target Incentive:	$16,000 ($80,000 × .20 = $16,000)	
		Outstanding Pay:	$112,000 ($16,000 × 3 + $64,000 = $112,000)	
5	Measures and Weights	Sales Volume:	100%	
6	Quota Distribution	Meet/Exceed Target: Below Target:	60%–70% 30%–40%	
7	Performance Expectations	**Performance Range**		
			Percent to Goal Revenue	
		Threshold:	75%	
		Target Performance:	100%	
		Excellence Performance:	125%	
8	Assign Pay Opportunities to Performance Expectations	**Total Pay Opportunity**		
			Components	Cumulative
		Threshold:	$64,000 (Base Salary)	$64,000
		Target Incentive:	$16,000	$80,000
		Excellence:	$32,000 (Outstanding Pay)	$112,000

		Pay Compensation by Performance Measure		
			Sales Volume	
		Result*		Pay
		Minimum:	75%	$ 0
		Target:	100%	$16,000
		Outstanding:	125%	$48,000
		*Sales results are expressed as a percent of quota performance		
9	Calculate Formula	**Bonus Formula Payout Rate**		

Express payout as a percent of salary range midpoint ($64,000)

To calculate the bonus formula rate, determine the value of each percent for below-quota performance and then for above-quota performance.

Below-Quota Performance. Calculate the payout rate for below-target performance:

$$\frac{(\$80,000-\$64,000)/\$64,000}{(100-75)} \times 100 = 1\%$$

Above-Quota Performance. Calculate the above-quota performance payout rate:

$$\frac{(\$112,000-\$80,000)/\$64,000}{(125-100)} \times 100 = 2\%$$

10 Publish Formula

Base Salary Range

	Minimum	Midpoint	Maximum
	$60,000	$75,000	$90,000
Bonus Rate			
		For Each Percent to Quota	Pay a Percent of Base Midpoint
		0–74%	0
		75–100%	1%
		Over 100%	2%

Figure 6-20 Worksheet 4—bonus formula rate.

Figure 6-21 Bonus formula rate.

Worksheet 5: Bonus Formula Matrix

Use a bonus formula matrix when territories are dissimilar in size and the salesperson must resolve objectives on two competing measures (see Figure 6-22).

	Steps	Formula Parameters		
1	Total Target Compensation	$120,000		
2	Pay Mix	70/30		
3	Leverage	3×		
4	Pay Opportunities	**Base Salary Range**		
		Minimum:	$ 67,200 ($84,000 × .8 = $67,200)	
		Midpoint:	$ 84,000 ($120,000 × .7 = $84,000)	
		Maximum:	$100,800 ($84,000 × 1.2 = $100,800)	
		Target Base Salary:	$ 84,000 ($120,000 × .7 = $84,000)	
		Target Incentive:	$ 36,000 ($120,000 × .3 = $36,000)	
		Outstanding Pay:	$192,000 ($36,000 × 3 + $84,000)	
5	Measures and Weights	Sales Volume:	50%	
		Price Realization:	50%	
6	Quota Distribution	Meet/Exceed Target:	60%–70%	
		Below Target:	30%–40%	

7	Performance Expectations	**Performance Range**		
			Percent to Goal Revenue	Price Realization
		Threshold:	60%	92%
		Target Performance:	100%	100%
		Excellence Performance:	140%	108%

8	Assign Pay Opportunities to Performance Expectations	**Total Pay Opportunity**		
			Components	Cumulative
		Threshold:	$84,000 (Base Salary)	$ 84,000
		Target Incentive:	$36,000	$ 36,000
		Excellence:	$72,000	$192,000
			(Outstanding Pay)	

Pay Compensation by Performance Measure

	Sales Volume		Price Realization	
	Result*	Pay	Result	Pay
Minimum:	60%	$ 0	92%	$ 0
Target:	100%	$18,000	100%	$18,000
Outstanding:	125%	$36,000	110%	$36,000

*Sales results are expressed as a percent of quota performance

9	Calculate Formula	**Bonus Formula Matrix**

Establish the number of rows and columns
9 rows by 9 columns
Determine "penalty" for achieving one goal without achieving the other:

40% loss of target bonus for revenue and price realization

Set the corners.

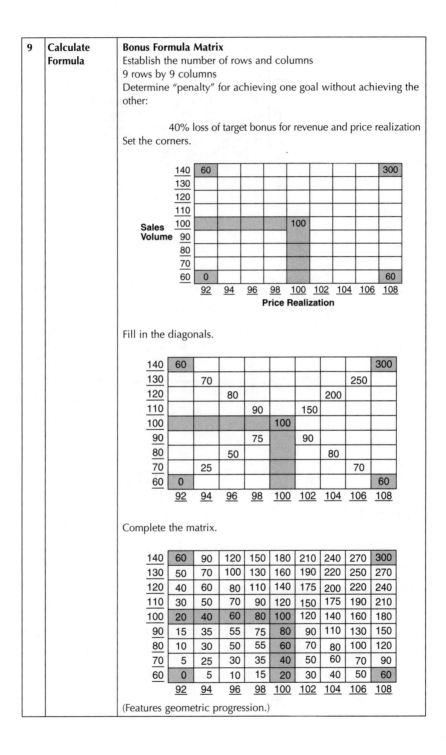

Sales Volume (rows) × **Price Realization** (columns)

Sales Volume	92	94	96	98	100	102	104	106	108
140	60								300
130									
120									
110									
100					100				
90									
80									
70									
60	0								60

Fill in the diagonals.

Sales Volume	92	94	96	98	100	102	104	106	108
140	60								300
130		70						250	
120			80				200		
110				90		150			
100					100				
90				75		90			
80			50				80		
70		25						70	
60	0								60

Complete the matrix.

Sales Volume	92	94	96	98	100	102	104	106	108
140	60	90	120	150	180	210	240	270	300
130	50	70	100	130	160	190	220	250	270
120	40	60	80	110	140	175	200	220	240
110	30	50	70	90	120	150	175	190	210
100	20	40	60	80	100	120	140	160	180
90	15	35	55	75	80	90	110	130	150
80	10	30	50	55	60	70	80	100	120
70	5	25	30	35	40	50	60	70	90
60	0	5	10	15	20	30	40	50	60

(Features geometric progression.)

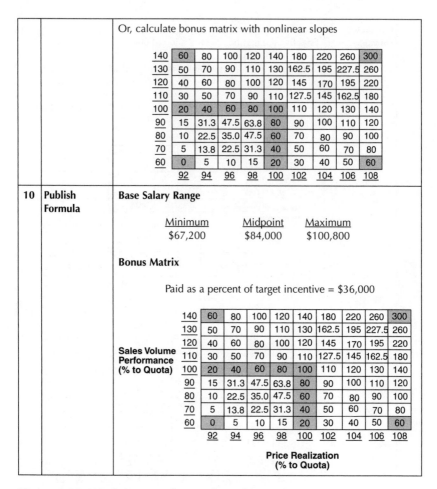

Figure 6-22 Worksheet 5—bonus formula matrix.

SUMMARY

The math is simple. Income producers get a percent of what they sell. Determine the preferred cost of sales and make that the commission rate. For sales representatives, determine what you want sales personnel to earn and how much volume they should produce, then simply divide pay by performance to get the payout rate.

Chapter 7

Support Programs: Territories, Quotas, and Crediting

Sales compensation programs function in concert with the following support programs: territory configuration, quota management, and sales crediting. Each of these mission-critical support programs performs an important sales management role. Collectively, sales compensation and these support programs form the backbone of the sales performance management system. Sales management needs to continually define, monitor, and revise these support programs to serve the company's evolving sales strategy. The success of the sales compensation program rests with the effectiveness of these interdependent programs. Consequently, when redesigning the sales compensation program, sales management must also review and revise these support programs.

Briefly, each of these support programs can affect the sales compensation program including scope of responsibilities, performance commitment, and achievement measurement in the following manner:

- *Territory configuration:* Territory configuration defines sales territories—"scope of responsibilities." The territory configuration policies provide rules for account assignment and reassignment.

- *Quota management:* Quotas define performance expectations—"performance commitment." Quota management encompasses two activities: quota allocation and quota adjustments.
- *Sales crediting:* Sales crediting defines sales success—"achievement measurement." Sales crediting specifies to whom and when individuals earn sales credit for compensation purposes.

The material that follows examines territory, quota, and sales crediting practices for sales representatives, but not for income producers. While some of these concepts do apply to income producers, they have a more limited application. So, our focus is on sales representatives—those who can earn and exceed a target incentive for sales performance.

TERRITORY CONFIGURATION

Sales management assigns accounts to territories for sales coverage purposes. The best performing sales organizations structure territories with homogeneous buyer populations making it easier for sales personnel to identify customer needs, deliver sales messages, and guide customer decision-making.

Because sales personnel receive incentive compensation payments for territory sales performance, we will examine how initial territory configuration and account reassignment practices affect sales compensation effectiveness. We will begin with a review of the most prevalent territory types. Then we will examine practices for making account changes mid-year, an area that needs watchful governance.

Configuring Effective Sales Territories

The art of configuring effective sales territories requires superior interpretation of company business strategy, rigorous analytical investigation, and studied judgment about customer needs. The objective of effective territory design is clear: create sales territories with the best return on sales investment dollars. This means optimizing dozens of trade-offs to arrive at the optimal territory design so that profitable revenue production is high and sales costs are low. Some sales organizations invest substantial resources in gathering market information and performance yield data to construct advanced analytical-based territory optimization models. Others find the variables so complex or resources so limited; they make their best guesstimate of the right territories and then make real-time adjustments as performance unfolds. Finally, others maintain historical territories as a rational approach if business conditions remain unchanged, but this is a risky position when sales conditions *are* changing.

For sales representative jobs, sales management attempts to provide balanced (equally challenging) territories by using different job titles. In this manner, sales management seeks to configure territories of equal opportunity so incumbents have an equal chance to earn and exceed the target pay for the job.

In an ideal world, the sales territories would be equal on the following factors:

- Number and revenue of existing customers
- Number and revenue of potential new customers
- Amount of available selling time
- Extent of customer needs
- Customer accessibility: travel distance, sales access time

Of course, it's impossible to configure sales territories to create truly equal sales opportunities. There are just too many variables. Sales organizations generally attempt, as best they can, to provide balance to the selling opportunity through effective territory configuration.

Although territory balance is important, focus is more important. Sales organizations need to focus sales personnel to optimize the learning process and selling time. For this reason, sales organizations seeking focus and hoping for balance will configure territories using one or more of the following criteria:

- *Geography:* One of the most popular methods of organizing salespeople is by geographic area. Geographic territories assume the buyers are alike and one salesperson can handle all the customers within a geographic area.
- *Stratified/size:* Another method of organizing territories is by account size. In a stratified sales organization, one group of salespeople calls on large customers; another group calls on medium-sized customers; and a low-cost resource handles small customers. A stratified sales organization will most likely have both named-account and geographic territories.
- *Account status:* Another territory configuration method divides territories into two categories: noncustomers and existing customers. Sometimes called "hunter and farmer" territories, this configuration allows sales personnel to focus on one primary task: hunters who sell to new accounts and farmers who manage existing accounts.
- *Vertical/industry:* Grouping accounts by industry type (vertical) provides sales personnel with the ability to understand the unique buying needs of a group of similar customers. Examples of vertical/industry territories include financial services, telecommunications, and consumer packaged goods.
- *Product/application:* Another territory configuration method groups current and target customers into territories based on product or user application. These types of territories place a premium on sales personnel product or application knowledge.

- *Project opportunity territories:* Some types of selling are opportunistic and are based on customer projects. Instead of a defined, ongoing territory of accounts, sales management assigns these sales opportunities to sales personnel as they arise. Examples include selling equipment and services to support major construction and engineering projects. Sales management defines the territories as a summation of these assigned major projects.
- *Hybrid:* Many sales organizations use a mix of territory types, even blending one or more together to achieve optimal sales coverage.

Optimal territory configuration uses sales resources efficiently. From a sales compensation perspective, effective territory configuration provides equal sales opportunities to all sales personnel in the same job. While this does not mean identical sales opportunity, it does accommodate the less exacting objective of comparable sales opportunity. *Comparable* means sales personnel view the sales challenge among territories to have relative trade-offs, and sales personnel in one territory are not significantly advantaged or disadvantaged by territory configuration.

Vocabulary Alert: "Geographic" and "named" account territories often coexist. Geographic defines territories in spatial terms such as region, state, county, zip codes, or manager-defined boundaries. Named-account territories define territories as a list of accounts. These two terms, used together, provide ample descriptive context. For example, "Your territory includes all accounts with the following zip codes . . ." or "Your territory is this list of major accounts . . ." or "Your territory includes five counties in western Pennsylvania, less the named major accounts." Or lastly, "Your territory includes all major named accounts in Illinois."

Mid-Year Sales Territory Changes

Territory reconfiguration usually takes place at the start of the fiscal year along with the assignment of new quotas and the introduction of new sales compensation plans. Sales management, during this time, makes every effort to bring balance to the sales territories in order to optimize the return on sales resource investment. However, there are numerous occasions mid-year when sales management needs to reconfigure sales territories. These mid-year changes to territories can impact the entire sales force or occur on a case-by-case basis. Adding or removing accounts from a territory will most likely increase or decrease payouts. Minor changes in pay opportunity—either up or down—may be acceptable without making pay program adjustments. Sales management must provide explicit policies for addressing mid-year territory changes whether they occur on an across-the-board basis or as one-off changes.

Mid-year territory changes can occur because of a variety of practical business issues:

- *Strategic focus change:* A company may require a reconfiguration of territories if the strategic focus changes regarding products or customers.
- *Staffing changes:* Changes in staffing levels, either increases or decreases, will affect sales territory definition. These changes may be caused by economic prospects, either positive or negative, or by mergers and acquisitions.
- *Customer changes:* Customer openings, relocations, and closures will change the census of customers within a territory.
- *Customer request:* Occasionally, customers may request a change in sales personnel (not a high vote of confidence for the salesperson).
- *Temporary changes:* When sales personnel are terminated or when a salesperson cannot cover his or her accounts because of

vacation, illness, or temporary assignment, others may be asked to temporarily assume account responsibilities.

Sales Compensation Policies and Territory Changes

Sales management should strive to avoid mid-year changes to the compensation plan. However, in some cases where major territory changes occur, sales management will need to make adjustments.

The following are sample policies for mid-year territory changes.

- *"No changes will be made to the compensation program or quotas if the territory changes affect less than 15% of the performance opportunity."*
- *"There is no retention of any historical sales or revenue credit when an account moves from one territory to another. In no case will two sales personnel receive credit for the same account."* (See "Sales Crediting," starting at the bottom of page 162.)
- *"For target incentive commission plans, if the territory changes affect more than 15% of the performance opportunity, declines of greater than 15% will be protected with a guaranteed minimum payment. If performance opportunity increases greater than 15%, the dollar amount where progressive ramps increase will be adjusted upward by the estimated percent of performance opportunity expansion."*
- *"For target incentive bonus plans, if the territory changes affect more than 15% of the performance opportunity, the quotas will be adjusted to match the expected increase or decrease in performance opportunity."*

Precluding Account Reconfiguration Abuses

In rare cases, unscrupulous sales personnel, sometimes in collusion with sales management, can manipulate the account assignment practices to inflate earnings. The sales compensation program should have a clear statement of consequence for any type of manipulation of the compensation program at the expense of the company.

Sales management should monitor the account assignment practices for the following types of abuses:

- *Quota relief:* Removing an account from a territory, in some companies, automatically lowers the quota. This technique is applicable when a customer's status changes, such as when a facility closes. However, a dishonest practice removes the account from the territory not because of legitimate customer status changes, but because sales performance for the account is so poor. The salesperson gets a free ride by having the quota reduced for poor performance.
- *Upside benefit:* In another twist, assignment of an account to a territory to benefit a sales representative without increasing the quota is another form of manipulation. Local sales managers sometimes assign such accounts temporarily or permanently to a sales person allowing higher pay to be earned against the (incorrectly) unadjusted quota.

It is best to keep mid-year account changes to a minimum. Any account assignment changes should have several levels of approval. All such changes should be visible and available on regular monthly reports showing the extent and impact of account changes by person for the period (monthly or quarterly) and the cumulative impact on the company on a year-to-date basis.

QUOTA MANAGEMENT

Quota management includes two components: quota allocation and quota adjustments. As with account configuration, quota allocation—the establishment of individual quotas—should occur at the start of the fiscal year. There are numerous techniques for allocating quotas, and we will examine several of the more popular methods. Quota adjustments occur during the year and for numerous reasons. We will look at these instances and provide guidance on how to address mid-year quota changes.

How Quotas Affect Sales Compensation

The impact of quotas varies depending on the type of sales compensation plan. For income producers with a flat commission, a quota might be merely a symbolic point, marking expected performance but without any financial impact. Also, quotas might be a point where the commission rate changes or is an important milestone affecting the relationship between the income producer and the company.

Quotas play a more important role for sales representatives as compared to income producers. Sales management uses quotas to distribute the corporate sales commitment to all sales personnel. For these target incentive plans, both commission and bonus formula, the target quota defines the degree of difficulty where two-thirds of sales personnel will exceed this number and one-third will not. For formulas with ramps (progressive or regressive), the quota will provide one of the break-points where the formula rate changes.

For target incentive commission plans, the average territory quota provides the calculation basis for establishing the commission rate. For target bonus incentive plans, quotas play a pivotal role in equalizing the earning potential of dissimilar-sized territories. Additionally, in target bonus incentive plans, the quota is an integral part of the payout formula. For this reason, quotas must be accurate—if they are too easy, the plan will overpay; if the quotas are too difficult, the plan will underpay.

Vocabulary Alert: Companies use words like *forecast, plan, goal,* and *quota* differently. However, in all cases, these words describe objective-based numbers. In some companies, management uses these words interchangeably; in other companies, each of these words has a specific meaning. However, most companies use *forecast* and *plan* (a noun, as in the business plan) to describe a companywide commitment. "The forecast for the coming fiscal year is to hit $875M in sales." Or "Our plan is to achieve $875M in sales." On the other hand, both *goal* and *quota* usually describe performance objectives for individuals or sales teams. "Your quota for your territory is $2.6M." Sales forecasting establishes a company's overall sales objective and quota allocation distributes the forecast to sales personnel as individual quotas.

Quota Allocation

Companies have numerous quota allocation methods to distribute the company's forecast to sales personnel. Quota allocation methods feature a combination of analytical tools and process methods. Regarding analytics, some quota allocation methods make scant use of market potential data and simply use last year's performance as the basis of this year's quota. Others invest significantly in measuring territory potential, territory market share, account growth rates, and account intelligence to create advanced analytical models for allocating quotas. From a process perspective, similar extremes exist. In some companies, sales personnel are not involved in the quota allocation process and simply receive an assigned quota number. In other companies, extensive field involvement in the quota allocation process includes active participation of sales personnel and field sales management.

The most popular quota allocation methods are as follows:

- *Top down/algorithm:* For industries where the product sales growth is tied to economic cycles and there are numerous customers (too many to know individual buying practices), the top down/algorithm method is the best quota allocation method. Management uses historical data and economic projections to create a mathematical model, an algorithm, to allocate quotas.
- *Top down/negotiated allocation:* Another method brings organization peers together to negotiate quota allocation decisions. The vice president (VP) of sales meets with his or her regional managers (RMs) to allocate the VP's quota among the RMs. Regional managers then meet with their respective direct reports, the district managers (DMs). Working with the district managers, the RM then allocates his or her number among the DMs and the process continues down the organizational chart until the process fully allocates all the forecast to individual sales personnel.
- *Top down, bottom up:* A third method features parallel activities of top-down quota allocation and bottom-up quota estimates. This process creates two quota allocation views. A reconciliation process at each level helps align these two quota allocation estimates.
- *Account planning:* Territories composed of a few large accounts use account planning methods to set quotas. Major account sales personnel are the best qualified to help construct a sales estimate for their large customers. Assembling a customer business plan, the major account manager presents this sales estimate to senior sales management for review and adjustments. The outcome of this planning and review process produces a quota for the large named-account territory.

Most companies need to use a combination of quota-setting methods to fully allocate the company forecast.

HANDS-FREE QUOTAS

An alternate method to assigning quotas is not to assign quotas. Known as "hands-free" quotas, no attempt is made to make individual quota allocation assignment. Instead, actual sales performance creates a percentile rank-order of the sales personnel. A formula provides payouts of the target incentive amount depending on percentile ranking. In this manner, there are no quotas. However, this approach has several noteworthy shortcomings. First, sales management compromises its leadership charter by not providing a meaningful performance goal for the organization and for individuals. Second, individual sales personnel have no idea how they are performing until after the ranking. They must wait for their individual percentile ranking. Lastly, it creates an internally competitive atmosphere where sales personnel knowingly compete against one another.

Special Issues in Quota Allocation

The following present special challenges to quota allocation:

- *Overassignment/underassignment:* Some sales management teams intentionally overassign or underassign the forecast during the quota allocation process. Overassignment occurs when the summation of individual quotas exceeds the overall forecast objective. Sales leaders who advocate this practice believe the extra cushion helps ensure that the sales team will make its number, given unexpected events such as customer changes, product issues, or turnover among sales personnel. Underassignment, sometimes known as breakage, is the opposite of overassignment. Sales leaders do not fully allocate the forecast. There are numerous reasons for this practice. The most common is to protect sales personnel from an unrealistic forecast created by corporate management. Another reason is to avoid the uncertainty of placing large unpredictable orders into individual quotas. In such cases, these uncertain large orders remain outside the individual quotas, but are often assigned to a sales manager.

For whatever reason, when sales leaders choose to overassign or underassign quotas, they run the risk of eroding their credibility or the credibility of the quota allocation process. At a certain point, sales personnel will learn that their quotas are not true quotas and therefore are open for adjustments, challenges, and compromise.

- *Seasonality:* Some sales cycles are very seasonal, peaking at different times of the year. If performance and pay periods align with these seasonal fluctuations, then sales management needs to assign seasonally adjusted quotas.
- *Market uncertainty:* Market uncertainty—potential high growth or significant declines—makes quota allocation more problematic. Two potential solutions exist: shorten the performance period or use rolling averages. If sales management does not have the market visibility to set realistic one-year quotas, then shortening the performance period for quotas can help. Instead of 12-month quotas, set 6-month quotas, or even quarterly quotas. Another method is to use a rolling-average quota calculated by taking the last 3 months of actual performance multiplied by an adjustment factor (plus or minus) to calculate the next performance period quota.
- *Long sales cycles:* Long sales cycles present another challenge for quota allocation. When the sales cycle is greater than 12 months, annual quotas become irrelevant. In such cases, it's best to move to an event-based incentive plan where payouts are tied to sales events such as contract signing and not quota performance.
- *Periodic mega orders:* Some sales models have a mix of predictable sales orders interspersed with unpredictable mega (large) orders. It's best not to place these mega orders into the quota; instead, provide a separate payout formula for these orders,

correctly applying a regressive rate above a certain dollar volume. This separate schedule is further enhanced by requiring sales personnel to register major deals. Without preregistering a deal, the incentive compensation available for such orders is significantly lower. This policy supports the following rationale: "If you had no knowledge of the order, then you did not have much influence on the purchase . . . ; therefore, your pay should be commensurate with your degree of influence . . . which shouldn't be much."

- *New products:* At the beginning of each fiscal year, product management may have a schedule of new product launches. Predicting with accuracy the launch of these new products affects the quota allocation process. If the launch dates are accurate and the sales performance expectations realistic, then sales management should include these new products in the quota. However, if the dates are not confirmed or the projected sales volumes are indeterminate, then exclude these new products from the quota. Give them their own launch incentive (an add-on) that expires at the end of the performance period. Then, when you have more solid information, include these new products in the quota for the next performance period.

Quota allocation provides sales leadership with an opportunity to manage performance. Quota allocation requires ongoing efforts from year to year to make adjustments and improvements.

Mid-Year Quota Changes

Most companies need to consider mid-year changes to quotas. Like mid-year account changes, mid-year quota changes require across-the-board adjustments, or case-by-case changes. Sales management seeks to balance quota fairness by achieving forecast commitment. While some mid-year changes cause an increase in quotas, many petitions for mid-year changes are the opposite, causing a reduction in quotas—with no commensurate reduction in earning opportunities.

Complex sales organizations often provide for mid-year changes, but limit the scope of such changes with restrictive policies such as the following:

- *"No quota change can be made unless the performance opportunity will be altered by greater than 15%."*
- *"Quota adjustments are considered for changes outside the influence of the salesperson, but excludes activities associated with customer-buying practices, market trends, competitor actions, company fulfillment, and company terms policies."*
- *"No quota adjustments can be made without commensurate adjustments to other quotas to offset the change, positive or negative."*
- *"Any quota adjustment must be approved by all regional managers, the chief financial officer (CFO), and the vice president of sales."*
- *"No quota adjustments can be applied retroactively and none can be made at any other time than the beginning of the fiscal quarter."*

While most companies will need to make quota adjustments, restricting quota changes enhances the importance of the quota and precludes excessive requests for dubious quota adjustments.

Making Mid-Year Changes

In some cases, sales management will need to make mid-year quota changes. The following are compelling reasons to make mid-year changes:

- *Major economic change:* Whether a dramatic positive upswing or a profound downswing in the economy, sales management may need to adjust quotas. For major changes in the economy, an across-the-board quota increase will recalibrate performance and payout expectations. A best-practice technique is to terminate the current plan, make all legally obligated payments under the current plan, and then begin a new plan with the appropriate adjustments.

- *Account changes:* Whether caused by mergers, acquisitions, reorganization, or account assignment fine tuning, make quota adjustments if the changes affect the performance opportunity by more than 15 percent.
- *Currency and pricing changes:* Changes in revenue value caused by currency fluctuations or company pricing decisions should cause a similar offsetting adjustment to quotas.
- *Acts of God:* Most sales compensation plans allow for quota adjustments caused by acts of God, such as major weather calamities.

In summary, some quota adjustments may be necessary, but restrict the practice to protect the integrity of the quota management process.

SALES CREDITING

Sales crediting specifies when sales personnel earn credit for a sale. We will examine sales crediting eligibility, timing, and adjustments.

Sales Credit Eligibility

Who should get credit for a sale? The answer should be simple: the salesperson—the person who closed the sale . . . right? In sales organizations with a single sales force, applying this eligibility definition is relatively easy. However, in more complex sales organizations with multiple channels, overlay sales specialists, and team selling, the definition of sales credit eligibility becomes more clouded.

There are three major categories of sales crediting:

- *Seller sales credit:* Simplify sales crediting by assigning it to those who have customer contact and can persuade the customer to act. The single seller who influenced the customer to buy should receive 100 percent of the sales credit. If two or more sellers influence the customer, then those sellers share the sales credit using a prespecified proportional split. In target-incentive bonus formula design, sales management can double credit both sellers, but each seller must have an identical up-lift in their quotas to offset the double crediting. In this manner, while sales crediting is double counted, it does not elevate payouts.
- *Vertical sales credit:* Vertical sales credit refers to the upward crediting of sales results through the field management layers. This is an acceptable accounting recognition practice. This is legitimate and is not considered to be double crediting.
- *Horizontal sales credit:* Horizontal sales credit provides sales credit to resources who are not the primary sellers. In a true economic sense, this form of sales crediting generates additional double costs. Sales management often uses this form of double crediting to support the field sales strategy. Sales credit is often awarded to sales support resources such as product overlay specialists and presales support personnel. For example, a regional product overlay specialist will earn sales credit for all sales in the region regardless of his or her involvement with a specific sale. Presales support specialists provide another example where double sales crediting supports the overall sales strategy. In both cases, sales management makes a conscious decision to reward more than one person for a sale. In these examples, horizontal sales credit promotes cooperation between sales personnel and those assigned to support them in the sales process.

Well-crafted policies regarding sales crediting eligibility will suppress some of the following sales crediting errors:

- *Landlording:* Sales personnel do not own accounts and therefore receive automatic sales credit for all products sold to the customer. Some sales might come from another sales channel independent of the salesperson. In such situations, sales personnel do not earn credit (as a landlord) on those sales, specifically sales they did not influence.
- *Appeasement pay:* Sales management will want the field organization to support a new channel, such as the telephone sales personnel. In an attempt to win the support from the existing direct sales channel, sales management incorrectly double credits both parties.
- *Annuity business:* The general rule is to "pay for persuasion once." Providing ongoing sales credit to sales from previous years, now covered by a contract and managed by the customer service department, is an ineffective use of incentive dollars.

Sales Credit Timing

Sales credit timing specifies when sales management recognizes a sale for incentive credit purposes. There are several points in the sales/ purchase process where this credit can occur. Assign earned sales credit to the salesperson at the point where the customer purchase is assured because you want the salesperson to stop thinking about the order. There are several points along the purchase continuum where sales management can recognize sales credit:

- *Product specification:* Certain industries recognize sales prior to a sales event. In purchasing components for their product, a customer will specify a vendor's product. Examples include design-wins for semiconductor sales or building materials specification for funded major commercial projects. Even though the customer has not issued a formal purchase order, the specification confirms that the order will be forthcoming. Some sales organizations accept specification for sales crediting purposes.

- *Booking:* An order is booked when a company accepts an order. Many sales organizations provide incentive compensation credit at the time of booking particularly if there is little likelihood of order cancellation, need for customer follow-up, or extensive installation support.

- *Invoice/ship:* Most companies ship products and issue an invoice at the same time. At this point, the accounting system recognizes the order as an account receivable. Use invoice/ship for crediting sales if there is a high rate (over 5 percent) of orders being changed or cancelled between booking and invoice/ship.

- *Installation/customer acceptance:* The next step in the purchase process is the installation/customer acceptance event. Major purchases often require a sign-off by the customer before they will pay the invoice. If sales management wants the salesperson involved in customer acceptance, then credit the sale at the point of installation/customer acceptance for sales compensation purposes.

- *Customer payment:* The final step in the purchase process is the receipt of the customer payment. Most companies recognize sales credit prior to this point, but for sales environments where customer payment is problematic, waiting until the company is paid before granting sales credit would be prudent.

- *Hybrid:* Some companies split the credit with 50 percent credit at booking and 50 percent credit at installation, as an example.

Sales credit timing should reflect the preferred involvement of the salesperson. As a rule: "Credit sales personnel when you no longer want them involved in the sales process."

Sales Credit Adjustments

Most sales compensation plans provide for payment on *net* sales, that is, less returns and sales credits. Sales personnel should not be paid for sales that are not fully realized by the company. Thus net-out (reduce) sales credit by any returns before calculating the incentive payment.

Additionally, some sales organizations also net-out past due receivables that extend beyond a fixed number of days outstanding such as 90 or 120 days. Once past this cut-off time, some companies deny sales credit even if the company eventually collects the money.

Paying on Sales-Out Performance

Indirect sales personnel with end-user business development responsibilities have a unique challenge to document sales credit for what they influenced. For example, sales personnel who sell personal computers and software through distributors and value-added resellers do not write end-user orders. Normally, they work with the distributor to help promote products through the distributor sales team. Additionally, part of their market development responsibilities includes making end-user sales calls. However, they do not write orders; instead, they refer the opportunity to the channel partners. The channel partners take and fulfill the order. Sales management of the manufacturer wants to reward their channel sales representative for driving end-user sales. However, the company does not have the information from the distributors to credit sales—which products were sold to which customers. This type of information is known as *sales-out* data. Of course, the channel partner has this data; but they are not inclined to share it with the manufacturing company. Why? They do not want the manufacturer to "take the line direct" and thus lose valuable customers. However, many manufacturers negotiate a financial arrangement with their channel partners to provide the sales-out data for either a fee or discount on the purchase of products.

Sales Credit Audits

Sales management should expect unexpected and sometimes unusual and out-of-policy sales crediting requests from the field sales forces. Mandate that no out-of-policy sales crediting can occur without senior sales management approval. Make the finance department your partner and schedule annual audits of sales crediting practices.

"Rolling Death"—a Union Negotiates a New Crediting Practice. The general manager of a telephone directory company was puzzled to learn that the business agent for the unionized sales force—a rarity in itself—wanted to lower sales personnel pay. The last contract negotiated between the company and union changed when sales credit would occur from payment receipt to the time of booking—a positive feature sought by the union. To protect the company, the new contract also added a companion feature requiring full commission payback if customers cancelled or reduced orders. Because of a high level of negative adjustments between booked value and actual payment, some sales personnel began to carry substantial payout obligations to the company. Known as "rolling death" because it carried over from one performance period to the next, many sales personnel wanted this provision removed from the contract and were willing to accept a pay reduction to accomplish this.

Preferred Solution: Because of the high number of adjustments between order and payment, the right solution is to go back to the previous practice of providing sales credit at the time of payment and not at the time of booking.

SUMMARY

Sales compensation works in conjunction with important sales management programs of territory configuration, quota management, and sales crediting. When undertaking a sales compensation redesign effort, sales management must examine these programs also. Large and complex sales organizations must be mindful not to allow these programs to contradict or negate the focus of the sales compensation plan. Policies and procedures governing these support programs need mindful attention. When properly aligned, all contribute to an effective sales performance management program.

Chapter 8

Difficult-to-Compensate Sales Jobs

Most sales jobs have easily assigned performance measures and goals. These jobs lend themselves to well-designed sales compensation plans. However, there are many difficult-to-compensate sales jobs. This chapter examines these kinds of jobs and offers possible solutions for consideration:

- Channel Sales Representative
- Long Sales Cycle, Mega-Order Sellers
- Business Development—Specification Sellers
- Strategic Account Manager
- Pursuit Teams
- New Account Sellers
- Account Manager
- Overlay Specialists
- New Hires
- Branch Manager
- House Account Manager
- Sell and Deliver Service Provider
- Merchandisers

CHANNEL SALES REPRESENTATIVE

A channel sales representative, sometimes called a channel manager, sells to channel partners who then sell to end-users or second-tier channel partners.

Issue: Most companies prefer to measure and reward the channel sales representative on "sales-out" revenue from the channel partner to the channel partner's customers. However, this is not an easy number to obtain. The channel partners need to provide this information to the company. Some partners see their customer list as a "trade secret" and do not wish to provide this information to their suppliers. Furthermore, to be useful for compensation purposes, the company normally wants this data at the outlet level. This number would allow sales management to reward sales personnel working with local outlets for their sales success. The less effective measure of "sales-in" to the channel partner can encourage excessive partner "inventory loading," which is not healthy for either party.

Solution: The preferred solution is to gather sales-out data from channel partners. This often requires persistent efforts, disclosure protection, and sometimes financial remuneration to encourage channel partners to provide this information. For those customers with multioutlets, compensate sales channel representatives for total sales volume and number of outlets reaching goal. A linked design would work best in this situation. While some channel partners may not give sales-out data on a regular basis, they may provide it on a periodic basis such as quarterly or annually. In such cases, the sales compensation program could grant an incentive award for the sales-out results after receiving channel partner information. However, absent sales-out data, sales management has a limited number of "fallback" solutions. The first of these less-than-effective choices is to measure "sales-in" data and provide an annual "resolution" bonus at the end of the year, using estimates of sales-out performance. Another approach is to organize field resources around channel partners. While individual outlet data may not be available, a team incentive on total channel partner performance could reward the whole unit. Finally, some organizations avoid using sales-in or sales-out data altogether, and instead measure product distribution and placement. For consumer packaged goods companies, *product distribution* is the extent to which the product is available through retail outlets. *Placement* describes the degree of favorable shelf placement of the product. Sales management can confirm and thus reward performance on these two measures with a combination of measurement techniques: self-reported, photo-evidence, and manager observations.

LONG SALES CYCLE, MEGA-ORDER SELLERS

In some companies, select sales personnel are responsible to sell large mega orders to customers who buy after a long sales process. These orders can range from multimillion dollars up to hundreds of millions of dollars of sales revenue. The sales cycle ranges from 12 to 24 months and longer.

Issue: Traditional quota-based sales compensation plans for long sales cycle, mega-order sellers are generally ineffective. Quotas are difficult to set. Order size and customer commitment dates are hard to judge. When attempting to use traditional sales compensation programs, sales leadership has to augment these programs with conditional statements, sales crediting limitations, and the use of caps.

Solution: If quotas cannot be set with certainty, then it's best not to use quotas. A better approach is to use a contract signing award. A contract signing award provides a reward at the time of contract close. The incentive program features a payout schedule providing increasing award payments for larger size orders. If the contract calls for future revenue recognition events, then divide the incentive payout between bookings and future payments or invoices. A traditional split would be 50 percent payout on bookings, and 50 percent on future invoices. If the order produces an ongoing revenue stream, then pay the contract signing bonus at booking and provide a step-down (i.e., declining) commission rate over the next 12 to 24 months. Finally, is "deal visibility" important at your company? Because of scheduling issues, most manufacturers need to have early visibility of any potential mega deal. In this instance, sales management can implement a "deal registration" program where sales personnel must identify all emerging opportunities. Registered deals receive the full incentive payout, whereas unregistered deals receive a more modest discounted payout.

BUSINESS DEVELOPMENT—SPECIFICATION SELLERS

Business development jobs influence customers to purchase, but do not actually write an order. Instead, the customer will place the order through a channel partner. Specification sellers are a type of business development sales job. Specification sellers influence engineers to "specify" the company's products in a final integrated solution. For example, heating and air conditioning manufacturers will attempt to influence architects to specify their units for a new apartment building. The new building owner or contractor will actually purchase the product through an authorized distributor. A similar sales process occurs with electronic component sales where the electronic sub-assembly seller will influence the engineering team to specify the company's unit. The sub-assembly company may not know actual purchase levels by the manufacturer if the manufacturer purchases these sub-assemblies from a qualified distributor.

Issue: It's difficult to reward business development—specification sellers on sales volume. While the company will know total sales and sales volume to specific channel partners, the company will not know precisely how the business development specification seller influenced these outcomes. In this case, individual sales volume performance is an ineffective measure for the incentive plan.

Solution: The challenge presented by business development—specification sellers is how to reward customer persuasion. Without being able to assign sales results to the business developer, only secondary measures are available for reward purposes. Some companies call these specifications "design-wins." A compensation solution might have the following design elements. Alternative #1, rewards sales personnel for achieving target design-wins. Akin to MBOs (management by objectives) or KSOs (key sales objectives), management can assign and reward target documented design-wins. Overall volume performance of the division can provide additional incentive earnings on a quarterly basis. For those sellers where actual sales volume can be tracked-back to a preregistered design-win, sales management can provide a modest commission rate for confirmed production. Deduct this payout from the company-wide incentive reward for total sales volume performance.

STRATEGIC ACCOUNT MANAGER

Strategic account managers handle the largest company accounts. Companies use various titles for this job including corporate account manager, enterprise account executive, and in some cases, key account general manager.

Issue: Strategic account managers' responsibilities don't easily lend themselves to quota-based sales compensation programs.

Frequently, the strategic account manager has one, possibly two accounts. Each of these major customers has unique account circumstances. No simple incentive formula can accurately capture the full range of responsibilities of the strategic account manager.

Solution: It's best to think of strategic account managers as business managers who manage external assets. As a company asset, these large customers require multiple resources to meet their needs. The relationship between the company and this large customer is often complex involving numerous parties, including presales support, customer service, contracts, supply chain, and procurement professionals. The strategic account manager acts like a "quarterback" to manage these mission-critical company resources. Strategic account managers should have a portion of their pay tied to continuing revenue, churn of existing business, and organic growth. The incentive plan should also reward success on preidentified "account initiatives" that increase utilization, penetration, and cross-selling. Finally, the strategic account manager should prepare an annual sales plan for each key account. Sales leadership should conduct quarterly reviews of these sales plans for major accounts and make appropriate adjustments based on evolving buyer needs. This sales plan should also describe the full range of customer support and engagement activities with the account. A typical split of the incentive component would provide 50 percent for growth of existing revenue; 35 percent tied to sales initiatives; and the remaining 15 percent tied to account sales planning and action outcomes.

PURSUIT TEAMS

Sales management will assemble pursuit teams to chase major opportunities. Sales management configures these pursuit teams based on customer buying needs. Often, opportunities arise quickly and fluid/flexible assignments are common with individuals potentially assigned to multiple teams.

Issue: Members of pursuit teams serve situational selling opportunities. These opportunities frequently arise in an unpredictable fashion. Classic quota-based sales compensation programs are an ineffective reward system for this type of selling. Quotas cannot be set. The sales role of team members varies from one selling opportunity to another. Assigning sales success is problematic.

Solution: Because these pursuit teams are collaborative, it's best to reward them on collective team performance. That means the incentive program will pay based on the sales division performance for the month, quarter, or year. Each role will have a target bonus opportunity. The compensation program provides target bonus opportunity payout based on total sales division results. Additionally, and as an option, individuals can earn special awards tied to exceptional sales contributions. Management or team members can nominate individuals for special award payments.

NEW ACCOUNT SELLERS

New account sellers have no existing account responsibility and spend their time converting non-customers to customers. Often they focus on the largest opportunities. Frequently referred to as "hunters," these sellers "catch and release." In other words, they "catch" new customers and "release" them to the account management team.

Issue: Most sales compensation programs reward for revenue performance. How is the best way to measure and reward new account sellers? Should the incentive program reward them for a number of new accounts, initial revenue, or future revenue?

Solution: The first step is to document the definition of a "new account." Because many accounts have purchased in the past, it's not unreasonable to define a new account as a customer who has not purchased in the last 12 months. Next, management must determine who can best secure the success of the new account. For example, if a new account needs to be "nurtured" by the new account seller, then the new account seller should retain account ownership until the account has reached a certain level of purchasing performance. A sales incentive can reward sales results from new accounts. At a predetermined point in the future—defined either by purchased volume or by some duration of time—the account manager then transfers the new account to the account management team. To facilitate this transfer the incentive plan can provide a "graduation" bonus to reward this transfer of accounts. A less preferred solution is to provide additional sales credit beyond the transfer date. This inappropriate approach can cause conflict between the new account seller and the receiving account manager. Next, if no additional sales support from the new account manager is necessary, then an immediate transfer to the account management team can occur. In such instances, the incentive plan can reward the new account manager for obtaining each new account, sometimes colloquially referred to as "landing a new badge." In this case, the incentive plan will provide an incentive from a new account payout schedule based on the estimated actual sales volume of the new account.

ACCOUNT MANAGER

The primary role of an account manager is to keep, increase, and penetrate revenue from assigned existing accounts. Sales management requires little to no sales results from new accounts.

Issue: A common mistake is to reward account managers for net increase sales volume to existing accounts. Unfortunately, this measure "masks" negative account volume churn. "Churn" is lost business. Additionally, existing accounts often provide the opportunity to increase volume from non-purchased products, new products, and sales to new purchasing centers within the existing account. However, protecting the existing revenue usually outweighs any additional incentives for penetration or new buyer selling.

Solution: To ensure balanced performance, the incentive plan needs to measure and reward strategic objectives such as account churn, product mix, and new buyer (within the account) revenue. To overcome the asymmetrical size of the existing revenue, the incentive plan needs to "modify" the revenue measure payout with success on one or more strategic objectives. For example, if reduced account churn of existing business is important, then the incentive plan can either increase or decrease the incentive payment from the primary net sales measure. This will ensure that the second, strategic measure of reduced account churn receives the full attention of the account manager.

OVERLAY SPECIALISTS

Sales entities use overlay specialists to support field sellers. Product overlay specialists work with the existing sales force to promote new and difficult-to-sell products. Market overlay specialists work with the existing sales organization in a similar fashion to assist sales to new and dissimilar vertical markets. Overlay specialists do not have assigned accounts. However, they do have a quota, either a product quota or a vertical market quota. Most overlay specialists are field-based and sales management assigns them to either a sales district or a sales region. Overlay specialists succeed when most of the assigned sales personnel are successfully selling focused products or opening new vertical markets. Sales leadership ultimately wants to retire the role of the overlay specialist as soon as all sales personnel can successfully sell the product or penetrate the target vertical market without the assistance of the overlay team. Of course, new overlay resources will emerge as new products or new markets need focused attention.

Issue: An incorrectly designed incentive program for overlay specialists rewards for total district or region's sales of the assigned product or market. This approach will encourage overlay specialists to work only with those sales personnel who most likely will help them achieve their assigned sales volume. The result is an uneven application of the overlay specialists' allocation of time. Instead of working with all sales personnel, the overlay specialists spend most of their time with the "big hitters" and not fully supporting the other sellers. This incorrect bias delays full adoption of the new products or vertical market focus by the field force.

Solution: To correct this misapplication of time by the overlay specialists, the incentive plan needs to reward both total sales and number of sales personnel achieving their goals for these focused selling accountabilities. An incentive modifier that increases or decreases the sales volume incentive as a result of balance performance among the sales personnel works best.

NEW HIRES

Sales management assigns new hires either into established territories or developmental territories. Sales supervisors expect these newly appointed sales personnel to quickly become productive achieving sales objectives.

Issue: Degree of sales difficulty affects the length of time needed for new hires to become productive. The compensation plan should reward sales performance, but not be overly harsh on new hires causing earnings duress. If the compensation program has a shallow base salary, and the length of time to acquire and close customers is lengthy, then new hire turnover might be greater than anticipated.

Solution: Several choices exist for providing "start-up" pay for new hires:

- *Choice #1: No Guarantee.* If sales management assigns the new salesperson to an existing or new territory, sales ramp-up time is minimal and base salaries are at least 70 percent of the target compensation, then there is no need for any type of guarantee.
- *Choice #2: Fixed Date Guarantee.* Provide a guarantee of 75 percent of target incentive for new hires when the base salary is less than 70 percent of the total target compensation and territory ramp-up time is minimal. Have this guarantee expire at some fixed date in the future consistent with typical ramp-up time. If, during this period, the incentive earnings exceed the guarantee, then allow the salesperson to keep these additional earnings above the guarantee.
- *Choice #3: Step-Down Guarantee.* Use a predefined "step-down" guarantee for sales jobs with a more aggressive than 70/30 pay mix. A step-down guarantee automatically drops the guarantee in steps, usually each month, until there is no guarantee left. This can occur over 3 to 6 months depending on the expected ramp-up time of the new hire.

BRANCH MANAGER

A branch manager both sells and supervises. A branch manager will have a list of assigned accounts and will also supervise a team of sellers. This hybrid job must balance these two dissimilar activities.

Issue: Branch managers need to balance the time between their individual sales efforts and supervising their direct reports.

Solution: The sales compensation program must help balance these two responsibilities: individual and subordinate sales results. The incentive program should link these two measures together with a hurdle. A preferred approach is for the sales compensation plan to delay any accelerator above quota performance on any single measure until both measures have exceeded quota.

HOUSE ACCOUNT MANAGER

A house account manager provides sales and service support to accounts not assigned to a salesperson. A house account requires no persuasive selling. Sales leadership might officially assign these accounts to a house account manager, or to a senior executive.

Issue: House account managers often act like salespeople. However, they most likely devote most of their time to customer service issues, thus ensuring ongoing customer purchases. Often, house account managers have a sales quota, too. Normally, house account sales volumes are large; much larger than accounts assigned to sales personnel. If management provided a sales incentive plan to house account managers, then payouts might be excessive and disproportionate to their sales influence.

Solution: Because house account managers do provide some degree of ongoing sales contact, sales management should provide a modest incentive program. The pay mix might be 90/10 and leverage might be 2 × the incentive opportunity. The plan should cap payouts. Tie 50 percent of the incentive to revenue performance, and the other 50 percent to KSOs. An annual payment would be appropriate.

SELL AND DELIVER SERVICE PROVIDERS

Sell and deliver service providers promote solutions that the customer purchases and then delivers these services. Examples include lawyers, accountants, and consultants.

Issue: Since these professionals are selling, providing an incentive for sales results would be logical. However, they also need to deliver these services to their clients—to be delivered on time and on-budget. A sales incentive might distract these professionals from effectively working with existing clients.

Solution: It's best not to provide a sales incentive plan to these professionals. Rewarding billing hours or delivered revenue provides the right incentive to follow through with the effective delivery of professional results. In the case where the seller is not responsible for delivery and instead "hands off" these sold opportunities to an engagement manager, providing an incentive tied to the value of the initial project/engagement will compensate these sellers effectively.

MERCHANDISERS

Working for the consumer package goods manufacturers, merchandisers execute in-store activities that position and promote the company's products in retail outlets.

Issue: Some sales executives would like to provide an incentive to these in-store merchandisers for effective product placement, training of retail sellers, marketing research, and, in some cases, product demonstrations. However, sales management does not expect these individuals to sell.

Solution: Most consumer package goods sales executives do not classify merchandisers as sellers. However, providing a modest annual 90/10 incentive with a 2× capped payout opportunity can help reward various account fulfillment duties.

SUMMARY

For certain difficult-to-compensate jobs the most common problem is acquiring reliable performance data. This lack of data can compromise the effectiveness of sales compensation plans. As a result, sales management methods other than incentive pay may prove more appropriate.

Chapter 9

Compensating the Complex Sales Organization

Large sales entities often deploy complex sales models to address unique customer coverage challenges. These sales organizations require well coordinated and comprehensive sales compensation programs to effectively serve these distinct and unique coverage solutions.

Four major sales effectiveness principles drive sales force complexity:

1. *Align sales resources around buyer segments.* While operations within companies organize around product types, sales entities must organize around buyer populations. Customers' needs drive sales organization design. For example, large customers typically need sales solutions different from small customers. Some customers require long sales cycle selling, while others do not. Some customers buy many products, while some buy only select offerings. And, some customers may need more technical support, while others do not. These variations can be numerous and expansive. To start, each company should be able to articulate

these "buyer segments" and their economic worth to the company. Then sales resource allocation decisions determine how best to serve these "target buyer segments." The outcome is frequently a complex tactical assignment of selling resources. Sales force complexity increases as the number of products and buyer segments increases.

2. *Promote all products.* As companies grow their product base, sales organizations need to effectively sell and promote diverse product types. Often, the use of a single sales resource selling all products becomes a challenge. To ensure sales focus on all products, sales departments will employ a variety of methods to effectively sell the full family of products. Examples include such coverage techniques as dedicated product sellers, product overlay specialists, and presales support specialists. In addition to compensating these diverse sales roles, sales leadership sometimes employs special product incentives within the sales compensation program.

3. *Ensure sales coverage among multiple touch points within customers.* Customer buying decisions often increase in complexity as multiple parties become involved in critical and high-risk purchases. A company might deploy teams of selling resources to address the interests of users, technical design, operations, finance, IT, and purchasing. Some sales departments might need to duplicate these centers of interest at the customer by involving both corporate and local stakeholders. A sales organization needs to parse these contact points for sales coverage and influence purposes. The outcome can create numerous accountabilities, jobs, and teams. This sales coverage complexity presents numerous challenges to equitable compensation practices.

4. *Specialize to improve performance.* Task specialization is a natural bias when transactions and unit volumes increase. Sales leadership will divide the customer contact continuum into roles best

served by dedicated resources. Lead development might be handled by one group; another group might provide presales technical support; the seller might negotiate the close; and a launch-team might manage the implementation. Web-technology allows for seamless integration of vendor/buyer relationships for ongoing supplier solutions. Each of these roles, while necessary to improve productivity, adds additional layers of complexity to a sales organization and presents additional challenges to sales compensation programs.

All four of these factors move along as partially independent and partially dependent paths creating ever evolving sales coverage strategies within complex sales entities. Of course, the sales compensation plans need to migrate to support these emerging and shifting selling models.

EXAMPLES OF COMPLEX SALES ORGANIZATIONS

Is a "large" sales organization the same as a "complex" sales organization? Interestingly, "large" alone does not necessarily mean "complex." Some sales organizations are extremely large such as national real estate agencies or multi-level marketing organizations. These sales entities feature a high number of sellers but a comparatively simple internal sales model. Likewise, the sale of complex products does not necessarily mean that the sales organization needs to be complex. For example, while some large technology companies have very complex product offerings, they have a very simple sales coverage model.

Instead, complexity is an outcome of three conditions: a high number of dissimilar customer contact jobs; extensive interdependency among these roles; and overall high incumbent headcounts. As a number of highly populated, distinct selling roles increase and the extent of required collaboration expands, then the overall complexity of the sales organization increases.

The following direct channel sales models present increasing levels of sales force complexity.

- *Geographic sales coverage:* The geographic sales model is one of the simplest sales entities. Sales management divides customers and prospects into geographic areas. Sales management assigns a salesperson to each geographic area. The number of sales opportunities dictates the number of salespeople in the sales organization. More accounts mean more salespeople. For the most part, the selling activity is the same regardless of the sales territory. Geographic sales organizations are "simple" sales organizations.
- *Stratified sales force:* A stratified sales force features a sales coverage model tied to the size of accounts. Usually, strategic account sellers cover the largest accounts. Named-account managers sell to the middle tier of companies. Geographic reps handle the small customers. Telephone sellers might handle the smallest accounts. While these are dissimilar positions, their roles are clear.
- *Vertical sales units:* A vertical sales force organizes around market segments. Additionally, each market segment might feature a stratified sales model. While the number of sales jobs may be numerous, the overall complexity is still relatively mild.
- *Pre- and postsales support resources:* As product complexity and diversity increases, sales personnel may need pre- and postsales support resources. Presales support resources provide technical support during the selling process. Examples include providing product specifications, developing new solutions, and ensuring compatibility with customers' infrastructure. Postsales support resources include implementation assistance, user training, and issue resolution.

- *Overlay specialists:* Overlay specialists work with sales representatives. Product specialists have unique product knowledge. Product overlay specialists work with geographic, stratified, and vertical sales resources to promote specific product offerings to customers. Market overlay specialists possess unique knowledge about market segments. They work with assigned sales resources to successfully sell to unique buyer populations. Overlay specialists do not have their own accounts. Typically, sales management assigns them to a population of sellers to support the promotion of unique products or to sell to unique markets.

- *Dedicated product sellers:* Coexisting with the current sales force, dedicated product sellers focus on unique buyers to sell a specific product offering. Sometimes these dedicated product sellers work in concert with the existing sales organization; sometimes they work independently.

- *National accounts model:* A national accounts model requires two selling resources. The national account manager works with headquarter buyers to get approved as a qualified vendor. Local sales resources then promote the company's products to local buyers at the customer's facilities.

- *Sales teams—dedicated, situational, and virtual:* Select accounts might require dedicated sales and customer service teams. In such cases, the selling and servicing groups work as a team to meet customer needs. These dedicated customer teams adjust real time to customer requirements whether these needs relate to sales opportunities or service issues. An example of a dedicated team is a paired "inside/outside" resource. These teams feature a dedicated premise seller who makes periodic visits to the customer site and a second dedicated telesales resource who promotes purchases, handles questions, and takes orders. The second team model—situational sales teams—assembles the right resources to pursue a unique customer opportunity. Sometimes known as "pursuit teams," these temporary sales entities work together to close major opportunities. Customer needs drive team composition. A team could have almost any mix of members: sellers, executive leaders, customer service personnel, contracts, supply chain specialists, pre- and postsales resources, and overlay specialists. The third type of team is a virtual sales team. A virtual sales team appears to the customer as a seamless group of knowledgeable people working on their behalf. However, the only internal linkage these team members have is a shared data base. Examples include 800 numbers or Internet sales support that pull customer selling information from CRM (customer relationship management) data files just-in-time to meet the customer's needs. Intelligent account information helps the next contact person to move along the sales process. Virtual sales teams require a sophisticated sales management data system.

- *Disaggregated selling accountabilities:* Perhaps the most difficult to manage sales entities feature disaggregated sales responsibilities. In such sales models, the selling steps are broken into process functions and assigned to various resources. For example, a market development teleforce might develop leads. The sellers would present alternative solutions. A pricing group might prepare bids. A service group might specify solution implementation. An executive team might be responsible for customer commitment. An implementation task force might provide on-site rollout support. Each of these groups has some aspect of the sales process.

Of course, the most complex direct sales organizations use a combination of these selling models.

Similar levels of increasing complexity exist for indirect channels, too. Indirect sales entities sell through channel partners. These channel partners could be OEM manufacturers, distributors and wholesalers, systems integrators, value-added resellers, independent reps, authorized dealers, retail channels, and joint venture partners.

- *Independent representatives:* Independent representatives are an example of a simple indirect sales model. These "reps" promote the company's products to their customer base. They don't purchase the product, but instead represent the product on behalf of the company. Often organized by territories or regions, these sellers may sell the company products on an exclusive or non-exclusive basis. Exclusive agents/reps only sell the company's offerings. If they sell additional lines of products, they do not compete with the company's offerings. Non-exclusive reps will sell the company's products plus also carry competitor lines. Examples of this include insurance brokers who may represent multiple insurance underwriters. An independent rep organization can become more complex if the company decides to organize the rep organization by account type, volume, geography, product, or market.

- *Central decide/central buy models:* Some large channel partners operate central decide/central buy models. These customers make purchase decisions at their headquarters and distribute the product to their outlets with minimal outlet influence. To work successfully with a central decide/central buy customer requires investing dedicated selling resources at the customer's headquarters. For example, large numbers of consumer packaged goods companies maintain sales offices in Bentonville, Arkansas, to serve Wal-Mart who acts in this manner.

- *Multioutlet partners:* Multioutlet partners require sales support at both the customer's headquarters and local outlets. In such sales models, the local outlets require on-site sales support. For example, in the retail channels, there may be local opportunities for better product placement, co-op advertising, and promotions. While the headquarters' salesperson facilitates the overall account strategy, the outlet's sales personnel provide the local influence where opportunities exist.

- *One-stage and two-stage distribution channels:* One-stage distribution channels feature partners who purchase and sell to end-users. A two-stage distribution channel has master distributors who sell to local distributors. The local distributors then sell the product to end-users.
- *End-user pull sellers:* Companies that use channel partners sometimes deploy end-user pull sellers. These sellers will call on end-users to promote the company's products but will refer sales opportunities to the channel partners. These end-user sellers act as "force multipliers" for the channel partners.
- *Business development/product specification resources:* Business development resources influence intermediaries to specify end-users' purchases. Examples include pharmaceutical sellers (detailers) and sellers who call on design engineers and architects.
- *Joint partners:* Joint partners combine service offerings to provide customer solutions. Representatives from both companies jointly promote the combined product/service offering to potential buyers.
- *Partner/competitor relationships:* In some rare instances, a partner can also be a competitor. Independent software systems integrators may find they are competing with the in-house integration teams of the software vendor. Management of this acknowledged, but unavoidable embedded conflict requires a shared and documented understanding of "account ownership" and "customer buying preferences."

Finally, the most complex sales entities will have both direct and indirect sales channels and perhaps numerous subconfigurations as presented above. (We address the conditions facing global sales organizations in Chapter 10, "Global Sales Compensation."

CHALLENGES FOR SALES COMPENSATION

The management of complex sales entities requires careful sales strategy planning. Complex sales entities provide numerous challenges to effective sales compensation programs. Without proper management, complex sales entities can exhibit some of the following negative conditions:

- *Role confusion:* Complex sales entities have many sales and service roles. A poorly designed sales compensation program could inadvertently cause role confusion among these various jobs. Sales management must map all sales compensation components to align with well conceived sales and service accountabilities.

- *Channel conflict:* Channel conflict occurs when two or more sellers assume accountability for the same buyer at the customer. Poorly defined account ownership rules can quickly escalate to distracting internal conflicts. Worse, these conflicts can negatively affect customers' buying preferences by manipulative sellers.

- *Excessive sales crediting:* Without fully specified sales crediting practices, sales compensation plans are prone to excessive costs as numerous incumbents claim and earn sales credit for sales events they may or may not have influenced. Excessive double crediting is a common problem for complex sales organizations.

- *Costly administration:* Complex sales organizations have a tendency to create "complex" sales compensation with more than 3 measures and elaborate channel conflict rules and extensive sales crediting practices. As a result, the administrative burden to manage the sales compensation program can increase dramatically in terms of headcount, IT support, and overall costs.

- *Unintentional staffing shifts:* Uncoordinated target pay levels and varied incentive opportunities among jobs can cause premature or unintentional staffing shifts. Unless carefully managed, sales personnel, if allowed, will migrate to better pay opportunities through internal transfers.

PREFERRED SALES COMPENSATION OUTCOMES

Sales leadership of complex sales entities want their sales compensation programs to achieve these outcomes:

- *Meet customer needs:* The whole purpose of deploying numerous selling resources is to meet customer buying needs. Account assignments should be clear. The sales compensation plan should encourage behavior that places the needs of the customer first and internal interests second. The sales compensation plan should help avoid channel conflict.
- *Motivate to exceed sales objectives:* Sales compensation plans, regardless of the complexity of the coverage models and processes, should encourage the sales personnel to reach and exceed sales objectives. Overly complex sales compensation plans with confusing sales crediting practices—a weakness found in complex sales entities—need sales management oversight to avoid de-motivating seller distractions.
- *Promote internal equity and fairness:* With so many different types of selling roles, the compensation program must promote internal equity among the different selling roles. The logic of earning levels, quota assignments, and payout formula must share a consistent approach based on job scope, market practices, and sales production results.
- *Manage costs:* Finally, the sales compensation program must responsibly manage sales compensation costs. Sales crediting practices need to avoid incorrect sales crediting and needless

double crediting, which both increase sales compensation costs.

SALES COMPENSATION RULES FOR COMPLEX SALES ENTITIES

As sales force complexity increases, so does the sales compensation program. Some of the conditions created by the complexity will remain "chronic" without definitive sales compensation resolution. Instead, some residual conditions of role confusion, channel conflict, excessive crediting, and administrative burdens will continue and need active, situational management to mitigate the most adverse impact on the sales compensation program. The following principles will help support effective application of the sales compensation plans for complex sales entities:

Principle #1: Charter a Sales Compensation Oversight Committee

For complex sales organizations, appoint a sales compensation oversight committee. Without such an oversight committee, various sales leaders will take it upon themselves to make changes to re-design plans, interpret policies, make program modifications, change administrative protocols, and apply exceptions where needed. Unfortunately, what seems, at the time, to be a logical change or beneficial re-interpretation of current practices can unwittingly cause payout problems or establish a new, unacceptable legal precedent. The solution is to create a sales compensation oversight committee comprised of sales leaders, finance, product marketing, and HR. Committee membership should represent all sales channels and all incentive-eligible jobs. This committee can bring sound and comprehensive decision-making to program design and management.

Principle #2: Ensure Channel Neutrality

Sales compensation practices should not encourage sales personnel to force customers' purchases into one sales channel over another. Customer buying preferences should determine customer fulfillment practices.

Principle #3: Align Performance Measures

Assemble a listing of all sales jobs with their performance measures displayed. Note the weight of each performance measure. Have the oversight committee carefully test the relationship among all performance measures for all jobs to ensure performance alignment.

Principle #4: Rationalize Earnings Opportunities

As with the exercise to examine performance measures, develop a complete listing of all jobs, their target pay, mix, leverage, and actual earning practices among incumbents. Have HR provide market data to confirm target pay levels. Use the sales compensation oversight committee to make adjustments to target pay opportunities to foster internal equity practices.

Principle #5: Specify Sales Crediting Practices

Sales crediting practices should ensure that those responsible for successful customer persuasion receive commensurate sales credit. Sales leadership should anticipate any potential confusion over sales credit assignment. Minimize double crediting. Prescribe how sales credit splits work. Document, communicate, and enforce these practices.

Principle #6: Manage Account Assignment Practices

Like sales crediting rules, account assignment rules detail how and when field management can re-assign accounts and how quota treatment occurs when accounts change. These rules also describe how to handle in-process orders during personnel changes. Finally, document practices related to treatment of temporarily assigned accounts when territories are empty due to turnover or other personnel changes. Again, document, communicate, and enforce these practices.

SUMMARY

The use of sales compensation in complex sales organizations requires careful attention to detail, including design, application, and administration of the pay programs. Sales compensation designers must fully account for the interdependency of sales jobs within complex sales entities. These interdependencies will influence the target total cash compensation of jobs, the selection of performance measures, the rules of sales crediting, and account assignment practices. Charter a sales compensation oversight committee to provide program design integration and informed governance.

Chapter 10

Global Sales Compensation

The world economy is increasingly becoming more global. Financial interdependency, expanding global brands, and rising cross-border trade are all evidence of how the commercial world will continue to become more and more integrated as a global economy. Occurring in parallel is the worldwide search for managerial best practices. Driven by an increasingly competitive global economy, exceptional managerial competencies are breaking free of geopolitical boundaries. Enlightened corporate leadership seeks to adopt management best practices regardless of location origin. Sales organizations are active participants in this evolving world economy and the parallel search for leading practices. These trends are affecting—in a positive manner—the use and application of sales compensation programs on a global basis.

THE PHILOSOPHY OF INTERNATIONALISM VERSUS GLOBALISM

An underlying philosophical argument between internationalism and globalism swirls among sociologists, economists, and management theorists that directly and indirectly affects the design of sales compensation programs. To understand the implications of these two competing points of view, it is best to describe their extreme positions. An "internationalist" finds, embraces, and protects local practices. Culturalism is a sacrosanct institution that justifies rejection of outside practices. Historical practices, local attitudes, and country legal directives re-enforce the need for cultural sensitivity and deference to local wishes. Internationalists consider the imposition of non-local practices clumsy at best, and ineffective at worse. The internationalist's philosophy distains global solutions.

At the other end of the spectrum is the globalist. A "globalist" sees the world as a connected entity. Best business practices are a universal construct. Capitalism provides the cultural platform for shared views and similar management practices. Minimal local variations to global approach must be pragmatically situational. Local management must use something other than "culturalism" and "past practices" to preclude implementation of global solutions. The rapid adoption of world practices in all management disciplines provides justification for the globalist's perspective. Of course, a globalist would find the protection of most local practices unnecessary, illogical, and distracting.

To compound the argument, both sets of theorists allow evolution of practices within their narrow frameworks. Internationalists will concede that local practices change and evolve as local circumstances change. Globalists agree that practices will change as global conditions change. Both acknowledge that their preferred model is not static.

Globalists favor universal global solutions; Internationalists favor local solutions: a global versus local paradox.

A popular catch-phrase at one time was: "think globally, act locally." This phrase attempted to capture the right balance between global practices and local practices. Unfortunately, "think globally, act locally" did not provide enough clarity of when to adopt a global practice versus a local one. As a result, it has fallen into disuse.

Of course, it's almost impossible to be a pure internationalist or a pure globalist. There are too many variations between these two extremes to settle on one approach. However, it's between these two views—the middle ground—where the thoughtful selection of management practices for a given company exists. Within every company you will find stakeholders and operatives arguing one point of view versus the other. Internal politics make good use of this division of views. Arguments on either side can leverage the virtues or pitfalls of either philosophy.

Sales compensation is one of the many management practices caught between these two competing views. An internationalist would argue that sales management practices are culturally specific to a country's markets, traditions, and sales processes. Forced use of any global sales compensation solution would conflict with the local sales management model. On the other hand, the globalist finds these local variations pretentious and unnecessary. The globalist company seeks to deploy a universal sales strategy. All sales management practices are uniform on a global basis unless otherwise proven locally ineffective due to market conditions. In such companies, sales leadership implements the same sales management solutions on a worldwide basis, including sales compensation.

SALES COMPENSATION—A LOCAL SOLUTION

Sales compensation serves as a local sales management solution. Absent any global input, local sales management craft compensation programs to align local sellers' efforts with local sales strategies, local management practices, and local legal requirements. Local sales compensation design solutions continue throughout the world today as the prominent driver of sales compensation design. This is a positive and appropriate application of sales compensation solutions. Of course, these well-designed local sales compensation practices are not static. Even absent of global influences, the natural maturation of local commercial markets will require changes to the sales coverage model. These job changes typically affect measurement and reward systems, too.

The following outlines local factors that affect the design of sales compensation solutions:

- *Societal customs and trends:* Social scientists find pronounced variations in human interaction based on multiple societal preferences such as collectivism versus individualism; hierarchy versus egalitarianism; risk-avoidance versus risk-taking; and relationships versus results. A society that favors collectivism over individualism will place less emphasis on individual sales incentives and more focus on group success recognized, perhaps, with a modest group incentive payment. Sales forces within strong hierarchical societies do not need aggressive incentives to manage the sales force. Sales management can depend on expected subordinate compliance. A risk-avoidance society fosters "execution excellence" without the need to encourage and promote individual discretion. Aggressive sales incentives work best when sales management encourages risk-taking. Finally, a "relationship-centric" society fosters positive feelings among parties. This need for "harmony" usurps the application of "result-centric" sales compensation plans. Also, the affiliation needs of these society members have employees rank the sterling "reputation of the company" as the primary reason for their loyalty, dedication, and hard work. In fact, in relationship-centric societies, employees consider aggressive incentive plans impolite.
- *Market structures, maturity, and business objectives:* In many parts of the world, commercial markets have unique structures. For

example, in many Southeast Asian countries, the use of partners to ensure good "relationships" requires a channel strategy and channel support jobs not found in other markets such as North America. In some Middle Eastern countries sales personnel may need to work more closely with government agencies than elsewhere. Additionally, all markets are in transition. Some markets are growing faster than other markets. Sales strategies will differ from one market to another. Growth might be preferred in one market, while sales leadership requires sales profitability in another market. As such, sales management needs sales compensation solutions that match local market structures, maturity, and objectives.

- *Embedded employment practices:* Compensation and employment practices vary from country to country. Examples include employment for life practices, extended vacation time, tax favorable perks, 13-month bonus checks, discretionary payments, termination rights, and base salary protection. Local accommodation of these practices varies. In some countries, compliance is uniform. In other countries, the company may or may not follow these local practices. The most important factor here is the extent of "disparate treatment." If the employees (salespeople) feel their company is making them endure "unfair" practices compared to their peers at other companies, they may elect to work elsewhere.

- *Legal requirements:* Sales management must follow local legal requirements. Legal requirements can come from many sources—commercial laws, regulatory rulings, tax code, employment law, and collective bargaining laws. Each legislative entity (country or region block such as the European Union) can promulgate laws in any and all of these categories. Local legal guidance is necessary to ensure compliance with these pay management legal requirements.

TYPES OF WORLD SALES ORGANIZATION

Multinational corporations operate sales forces across many countries and regions. Some of these sales organizations function on a global basis. The following are types of sales entities employed by multinational corporations:

- *Global sales organization:* The global sales organization has a single executive directing all sales activities on a worldwide basis. This model best supports a company with a uniform product portfolio selling throughout the world to other multinational companies with worldwide integrated buying processes, for example, those that can be found in the semi-conductor industry. Beyond the single global sales organization, a similar sales organization design has several LOB (line of business) global sales organizations, each with its own sales leaders. Companies with distinct product families use this multi-LOB global sales organization model to direct sales activities on a worldwide basis for their distinct business units. In both cases, the world sales leader often favors global solutions but will accommodate local practices based on market or legal requirements. Normally, global sales leaders are less inclined to accommodate local differences based on style, philosophy, or past practices. For managerial purposes, sales teams might be organized by country or region, but the sales leader expects them to use uniform practices, including sales compensation.
- *World region sales units:* Many multinational corporations divide the world into major regions, each with their own executive team, including a sales leader. Companies use a variety of grouping acronyms to segment the world regions: NA (North America), EMEA (Europe, Middle East, and Africa), APAC (Asia Pacific, or sometimes Asia Pacific and China), CALA (Caribbean and Latin America, including Central and South America), EU (European Union), and sometimes non-contiguous parts of the world such as BRIC (Brazil, Russia, India, and China.). Each world region sales executive generally adopts uniform sales compensation practices

(Continued)

(*Continued*)

unless local markets or legal requirements dictate otherwise. A variation on this model is to have a combination of both world regions and country-specific sales entities. For example, a large, predominately U.S. company might have a sales organization for the United States, but then use world region sales entities for other significant parts of the world. In some cases, additional countries might have their own carve-out because of the heightened focus the company places on that country. Examples include Japan or mainland China. As with global sales entities, sales districts might be organized by country or sub-region groupings yet use world region solutions to manage the sales force, including similar sales compensation plans.

• *Country sales organizations:* Today, it's increasingly rare for multinational corporations to have business units defined by a single country, except for the very largest countries. In these instances, the business unit leader has full management responsibility for all business activities within a country. Supporting this business's unit leader will be a country-specific sales leader. This sales leader will employ uniform sales management practices throughout the country, including a single sales compensation program.

Most global companies use either global or world region sales organizations. In these cases, uniform sales compensation practices most often transcend country borders. Finally, it's not uncommon to operate a "hybrid" model—some combination of the above choices. The sales compensation practices will follow these hybrid organizational practices.

GLOBAL TRIGGER CONDITIONS

Many multinational sales organizations employ some form of global sales compensation practices. However, the definition of *global* can fracture along different definitions such as LOB world regions (NA, EMEA, APAC, and CALA), or by customer buying type.

Consider the theoretical "local-centric" world corporation configured with independent sales teams in each country. Now, allow these local country teams to craft their own sales compensation plans. Remember, each job in each country could potentially have its own sales compensation plan. Further, if the company provides no design guidelines or best-practice competencies, unencumbered local sales leaders will design pay programs to meet their local needs. Most likely these plans will exhibit a lot of "custom" design flourishes—some justified, some inexplicable. The outcome will be hundreds, maybe thousands of different types of incentive plans. While this scenario is increasingly uncommon, the adoption of global sales compensation practices by multinational corporations is situational and generally emerges as a result of various global-centric "trigger" conditions, such as the following.

- *World customers:* Some customers operate without borders. They make purchases on a worldwide basis. They have buyer influence points throughout the world that work together as an integrated team. They expect their vendors to provide an integrated sales team to work with them. These worldwide sales teams, regardless of location, need to have a shared, aligned sales compensation program. Likewise, some customers have cross-country functional entities that need coordination of efforts. For example, the buy decision may take place in one country, but the "ship-to" and installation and support may occur in another country at a local factory. In this case, the two sales teams—the buying location sales team and the receiving location sales team—both need some form of sales credit sharing. While the sales compensation plans might not be "uniform" for these two sales teams, the company still needs uniform and documented worldwide sales crediting rules.
- *Multiregion, global sales entities:* The most prevalent driver of global sales compensation practices is the emergence of multiregion and global sales entities. The leadership of these units expects to achieve economies of scale, excellence of execution,

and deployment of best practices. They will charter a project manager or team to "rationalize" the numerous sales compensation programs found at the local level. They will seek uniform practices unless local market conditions or legal requirements require accommodation. However, the reason for "differences" must be compelling to justify exceptions.

- *Program effectiveness and fairness:* Emanating from the corporation's sales and marketing center of excellence, HR/compensation department, business process improvement group, or, maybe even, the CEO, comes a call for adopting sales compensation best practices on a worldwide basis. These initiatives confirm the need to implement better practices that are more effective and fairer to both the company and sales representatives. This effort helps oversee the design, implementation, and management of sales compensation on a worldwide basis. Solutions range from education sessions on best practices to the imposition of predefined plans.

- *Control, audit, and administration:* Usually in response to "out-of-control" diverse sales compensation plans, a control, audit, and administration effort will impose rules on sales compensation practices to help eliminate the most glaring problems.

GLOBAL SALES COMPENSATION SOLUTIONS

Global sales compensation solutions come in many flavors. Each approach offers some degree of consistency, effectiveness, and management. The solution selected depends on the company's objectives and expectations. Continuing global pressure might see the evolution of the sales compensation program through several of these solution stages. No simple formula exists to select the prescribed global sales compensation solution. Some possible solutions are described as follows:

- *Global sales crediting policies:* Global accounts purchase products on a worldwide basis. For these accounts, the sales event—where the point of influence occurs—and the "ship to location" may not be the same. Global sales crediting solutions provide direction on how to credit these sales. For example: (1) Double-credit the global account headquarters sales representative and the local representative for the same sale. Double-lift the quotas of both to reflect this double crediting; (2) Provide a fixed split, 50 percent for the headquarter seller and 50 percent for the local seller; or, (3) Use customer relationship management (CRM) software to identify and reward point of sale. Finally, if the account buys in a central manner, then place all sellers in a self-contained global account team. Reward all personnel for worldwide global account results.

- *Education of best practices:* Encouraging the use of best practices can take many forms. The least intrusive method is to provide an education on sales compensation best practices to your sales compensation stakeholders. Most local sales leaders seek to understand how to best fashion their sales compensation plans. A full-day education session on sales compensation can provide the right level of understanding to improve the design efforts of local managers. Books, webinars, and articles can help, too.

- *Corporate guidance:* Corporate resources can provide invaluable sales compensation help to world, region, and local sales entities. Providing corporate principles for eligibility, target compensation, mix, leverage, performance measures, performance periods, payment periods, sales crediting, account assignment, and quota management outlines the guidelines for creating sales incentive plans consistent with corporate expectations. An additional level of support describes the design steps for creating new incentive plans. A "design guide" provides a step-by-step method to create effective and corporate-compliant sales compensation solutions. Next, offering suggested designs for "platform jobs" is an enhanced level of corporate support. Platform jobs describe typical and expected sales jobs found among all divisions, across all locations. While entity or location management may use unique and dissimilar titles, the description of the platform job reflects the most common sales coverage solutions. Multiple suggested sales compensation solutions for each platform job provide a starting point—and maybe a preferred sales compensation solution for each platform job.

- *Uniform global solutions:* In some instances, a global sales organization may want to adopt worldwide sales compensation solutions. Two approaches exist to meet this objective. The first approach is to convene a global sales compensation design team. This team, representing worldwide locations, would craft sales compensation solutions to reward all sellers in all locations. The design team would also carefully consider local exceptions based on market conditions and legal requirements. This team could act as an ongoing "governance" resource to review, adjust, and approve sales compensation plans. The final method to achieve worldwide consistency is to create and to impose sales compensation solutions for all sellers regardless of location or market conditions. However, these plans would still need to comply with local legal requirements. Sales management seldom follows such a uniform and sweeping approach to sales compensation. Only the blandest of sales compensation plans "fit" all seller situations. Local market conditions require sales leadership to tune the sales compensation plans to local selling situations in order to be effective.

TRENDS IN GLOBAL SALES COMPENSATION PRACTICES

A recent study by The Alexander Group, Inc., found the following trends regarding global sales compensation practices. As

Table 10-1 Global versus Local Sales: Compensation Practices

More Global ↑	Program	Percentage				
		Global	Country	World Region	Combination	Not Applicable
	Design Principles	53.93	21.35	13.48	2.25	8.99
	Approval	52.33	19.77	16.28	3.49	8.14
	Formula	42.05	27.27	17.05	4.55	9.09
	Pay Philosophy	41.11	31.11	14.44	3.33	10.00
	Measures	37.65	25.88	20.00	5.88	10.59
	Job Grades	36.05	25.58	17.44	3.49	17.44
	Automation	32.56	25.58	17.44	5.81	18.60
	Quota Method	24.71	31.76	21.18	11.76	10.59
	Pay Mix	22.99	33.33	25.29	9.20	9.20
	Payout Admin	26.74	37.21	20.93	6.98	8.14
	Pay Surveys	21.35	39.33	20.22	6.74	12.36
↓ More Local	Quotas Assign	12.94	43.53	15.29	15.29	12.94

Source: Sales Compensation Trends Survey, The Alexander Group, Inc.

Table 10-1 displays, sales leaders want to address strategic issues such as "Program Design Principles" on a global basis, while they allow local sales management to handle more tactical issues such as "Quotas—for Sales Personnel" on a local basis. More than 85 large companies with sales forces located in more than two countries submitted survey responses.

SUMMARY

Use of global sales compensation solutions will follow the arc of multinational corporations adopting worldwide sales coverage solutions. In parallel, worldwide best practices also will contribute to the adoption of more effective—and similar—pay practices.

Chapter 11

Administration

Sales compensation requires attentive administration and, in some cases, powerful automation tools. When done well, effective administration acts as an unseen but indispensable program foundation. To be successful, the sales compensation program needs responsive headquarters administration and unerring execution. Support for the sales compensation plan by sales personnel is a combination of aspiration, compliance, and trust. Ineffective administration can quickly erode participant trust. Inaccurate checks, incorrect crediting, late payments, and confused reporting will expend a sales force's goodwill. As the performance periods unfold from weeks to months, from months to quarters, and from quarters to annual measurement periods, sales personnel depend on the administration system to provide an accurate statement of their performance, and thus, pay. Often considered a back-office function, under-resourced administration can cause significant dissatisfaction in sales personnel and, even worse, create field flare-ups where frustration is so high that sellers stop selling as they await resolution of their confused incentive payments.

In this chapter, we will examine the components and best practices of effective sales compensation administration.

ADMINISTRATION COMPONENTS

Administration is a combination of policies, procedures and accountabilities, automation, and reporting. While the exact configuration of these functions differs from one company to another, they are inescapable components of sales compensation administration. Effective sales compensation requires proper provisioning of the administrative function.

Once a design team has rendered its preferred design and the plan has been approved by senior management, it then moves into the domain of program administration. Program administration covers all day-to-day operation of the sales compensation program. The following components comprise sales compensation administration:

- *Policies:* Policies specify the rules associated with the treatment of credits, quotas, employment status, and formula calculations.
- *Procedures and accountabilities:* Procedures provide the action steps for program execution. Accountabilities delineate individuals responsible for various administrative functions.
- *Automation:* The scope of automation support depends on the complexity and intensity of sales compensation transactions.
- *Reporting:* Sales compensation reporting includes providing meaningful information to diverse audiences such as sales personnel, sales management, headquarters management, and administrators.

The following sections provide a brief overview of each of these administrative components as well as suggestions for good practices and what to avoid.

Policies

Sales compensation policies are just the opposite of what you would expect from a sales compensation program: They are dry and not very inspirational. Sales management must provide detailed policy statements. Use the following checklist to ensure that you have the necessary documented policy statements:

- *Account assignments:* How are account assignment changes made—under what conditions? What sales credit rights do sales personnel have after accounts move in or out of territories? When are accounts moved for temporary purposes? How should temporary assignment of accounts affect sales credit and quotas? What happens when external account factors affect account status such as when companies are moved, acquired, or shuttered? Who approves account changes?

- *Quota management:* How is quota allocation done? How can quotas be changed? What is the petition process for quota adjustments? How will quota changes affect incentive compensation? Who approves quota allocation assignments and quota assignment changes?

- *Sales crediting:* What is the definition of a sales credit for sales compensation purposes? Who gets direct credit for a sale? How is sales credit split? When can double sales credit be awarded? What happens if orders are changed or cancelled? How is customer late payment treated? How is customer nonpayment treated? What accounting system report provides the official point of recognition for sales credit? How are sales credit petition adjustments submitted? Who has final approval on sales credit changes and adjustments?

- *Program timing:* When are territories assigned? When is quota allocation done? When are program changes announced? When do they take effect? When are exceptions and adjustments considered? When is the cutoff date and/or time for performance period crediting? When will checks be issued? When will approved adjustments be reflected in the incentive payment?

- *Program interpretations, exceptions, and adjustments:* Who is responsible for program interpretations? What exceptions will be considered? Which types of exceptions will not be considered? What form do adjustments take?
- *Benefit program treatment:* Which, if any, benefit programs for sales personnel differ from other company employees? How are the following calculated: vacation pay, holiday pay, life insurance values, retirement contributions, 401K contributions and company matching portions, flexible benefit deductions, and stock purchase programs?
- *Sales expenses:* Which sales expenses are reimbursed? How do sales personnel submit expenses? When are expenses reimbursed? What documentation is needed? How is use of personal automobiles treated? What financial obligation does the salesperson carry for use of a company car? What does the company provide, for example, mobile phone, wireless e-mail, personal digital assistant (PDA), pager, laptop, high-speed access away from the office?
- *Employment status:* How is the sales compensation program affected by new hire status, promotions, temporary assignments, transfers, terminations, sickness, death, and retirement? How is pay affected by time devoted to local sales meetings, training programs, and national sales conferences?
- *Governance:* Who has final program authority for the sales compensation program? Who needs to approve changes, amendments, and exceptions to the program?
- *Rights and obligations:* What rights and obligations do sales personnel have under the sales compensation program? What are management's rights and obligations under the sales compensation program?
- *Personal integrity:* What personal integrity expectations does management hold for sales personnel? What are the consequences for not upholding these expectations?

While sometimes off-handedly referred to as "boilerplate," do not be fooled into thinking that these policies are unimportant or that they exist as an understanding. Every sales compensation plan document should contain a policy statement section covering *all* of the above topics.

"We are a small company with three sales reps. Do we need all this policy stuff?" Well, yes. Size and management style cannot abrogate your responsibilities to prepare clear and unambiguous policy statements regarding the pay plan. Without such clarity, you run the risk of unpleasant legal action at worst, and distracted, wary salespeople at best.

Procedures and Accountabilities

Procedures provide a step-by-step description of how to execute the sales compensation program. Numerous responsible parties contribute to making the sales compensation program a success. Prepare a workflow chart to communicate accountabilities and timing. Each of the following subjects should have its own workflow chart:

- Account assignment
- Quota management
- Sales crediting
- Data assembly and audit
- Incentive calculation
- Reporting
- Audit and assessment
- Exceptions and adjustments

The best documentation of procedures makes it possible for any individual to take over a task and quickly assume the duties

What ▶ / Who When ▶	Establish Forecast ▶ Sept 15	Allocate Quotas ▶ Oct 15	Make Final Allocations ▶ Nov 15	Load Quota Allocations ▶ Dec 1	Calculate Incentive ▶ Jan 15	Issue Checks ▶ Jan 30
Sales Management	Input		Approve			
Sales Operations		Administer Process		Confirm		
Field Management		Allocate				
Sales Personnel		Estimate				
Product Marketing	Input					
Division Finance	Finalize					
Sales Compensation Administration				Submit	Calculate Incentive	
IT Automation				Load		
Payroll						Issue

Figure 11-1 Quota allocation workflow chart.

with little disruption in execution. In other words, procedures and accountabilities describe who should do what when. Figure 11-1 is an illustration of a workflow chart for quota allocation. This only represents a stylized example. Complete workflow charts provide more detail. Detailed workflow diagrams provide a road map of procedure steps and accountabilities. Once approved, render these charts into action steps. Publish these procedure action steps for each administrative function.

Automation

Today's compensation administrator can choose from among many automation alternatives including: desktop applications, custom solutions, dedicated applications, and program suite options. The selection of the right automation choice depends on information processing needs and costs. Of course, as processing needs arise, so do costs—both direct (purchase price) and indirect (staff and field time) devoted to data input, processing, maintenance, and reporting. Automation needs are calibrated on two variables:

Figure 11-2 Sales compensation automation needs.

- *Complexity:* Jobs, measures, crediting rules, and mid-year program changes drive complexity.
- *Intensity:* Intensity reflects the number of incumbents, transactions, and duration of measurement periods.

Figure 11-2 illustrates the relationship among these variables.

Figure 11-3 illustrates how automation requirements differ by need.

Sales compensation administrators can select from among the following automation choices:

- *Desktop applications:* Use desktop applications such as spreadsheets and simple databases when information processing needs are limited. An assigned administrator keeps the desktop application up-to-date and loads the few transactions per performance period. Be careful not to incorrectly extend the use of desktop applications as complexity and intensity increase.
- *Custom solutions:* Whether developed internally or by an external vendor, custom solutions—those crafted to serve current information needs—allow users to have their needs exactly met. The advancement of software development tools has reduced the time to develop such solutions while increasing the power

	Limited	Moderate	Extensive
Conditions	Fewer than 50 Payees Few Jobs Fewer than 3 Measures Simple Crediting Rules Few Changes Few Transactions Quarterly Periods One Currency	←——→	More than 250 Payees Over 15 Jobs 10 Measures or More Complex Crediting Rules Frequent Changes Over 100k/Period Weekly/Monthly Periods Multicurrency
Functionality	*Manual Execution* Payout Calculation Manual Control Payroll File Limited Reporting	←——→	*Hands-Free Execution* Input Audit/Cleansing Linked Input Loading Automatic Processing Automatic Status Updates Multireporting Modeling Tools
Data Input	Manual Entry Manual File Transfer Single Data Source No Data Cleansing	←——→	Automatic Feeds Numerous Sources Data Reconciliation Multiperiod Tracking
Transaction Processing	Simple Calculation Limited Number Single Time Event No Past Reconciliation No Credit Splits	←——→	Numerous Calculations Complex Calculations Multitime Periods Numerous Reconciliation Multiple Credit Events High Transaction Count
Maintenance	Few Changes Few Adjustments Limited Updates Stable Quotas Stable Work Force Stable Territories	←——→	Many Changes Many Adjustments Extensive Plan Updates Changing Quotas Changing Work Force Changing Territories History Files
Data Output	Payroll File Management Reports	←——→	Input Audit Report Exception Reporting Management Reports Incumbent Web Reports Assessment Reports Payroll File Trend Reporting
Cost Modeling	None	←——→	Plan Change Impact Multivariable Scenarios Sensitivity Testing Market Data Calibration Optimization Choices

Figure 11-3 Various automation needs.

and flexibility of the application. However, changes will require software engineering support.

- *Dedicated application:* Numerous vendors now provide dedicated incentive compensation application software. These products are evolving and range from extremely powerful (and sometimes confusing) to very simple (but with limited capability). Two categories exist: stand-alone solutions that operate as unique applications and bundled solutions that are part of other front-office software suites.

Finally, the sales compensation administrator can choose from several service models:

- *Installed solution:* An installed solution is the most common service model. Using this approach, a company builds or buys a software application and runs the application on the company's own information technology (IT) system.
- *Hosted solution:* A second service model is to have the application hosted by a third-party vendor that provides data access and information processing via Web links or electronic data transfer methods. This approach helps reduce the burden on internal IT resources.
- *Outsource:* The third choice is to purchase outsourcing support where a third-party vendor provides the complete solution—both application and administrative support. Companies who wish to remove administration completely should purchase this type of service.

Reporting

With rapid advances in information systems and Internet communications, a more expansive palette of reporting choices is now available:

- *Administrator reports:* Administrators need ongoing reporting of program operation as regular production cycles occur: input audit reporting, exception tracking, and current status (organizational reporting, credit assignments, territory assignments, and quota assignments).
- *Senior sales management reports:* Sales leadership needs to monitor the effectiveness, cost, and results of the sales compensation program. Key indices of quota performance, payout levels, and product sales provide a "dashboard" of metrics.

- *Field sales management:* All levels of field sales management require immediate on-line access to current sales performance and trend information. Special reporting capabilities provide information for sales analysis purposes. Additionally, first-line supervisors use detailed sales performance information to help coach individual sales representatives.
- *Product management:* Product management examines product sales information by various factors to gain insight on how to best support the field sales organization.
- *Finance:* Finance accesses sales performance and compensation data to evaluate return on sales expense dollars, administrative compliance, and revenue and profit contribution.
- *Human resources:* Human resources gather sales compensation payout information to evaluate external competitiveness and internal equity.
- *Executive management:* Executive management evaluates the overall effectiveness of the program by reviewing summary analytical reports on program performance.

HOW TO AVOID UNNECESSARY ADMINISTRATIVE BURDENS

Without proper management, sales compensation programs can sometimes require unwarranted, elaborate, administrative systems and costly software solutions. To reduce unnecessary administrative burdens, consider the following recommendations:

- *Limit changes:* A certain number of changes need to occur during the program year but limit the number, extent, and scope of changes (quotas, territories, sales crediting, and formula calculation).
- *Exclude volatile and uncertain items:* Exclude from the sales compensation program factors that frequently change and treat

them separately. Examples include new product launches, uncertain mega orders, and special product campaigns.

- *Tolerate inequities:* In some cases, trying to keep the sales force whole can create excessive tracking and accounting issues.
- *Control exceptions:* Place a limit on what, why, and when exceptions will be considered.
- *Limit credit splits:* Limit the use of credit splits and double crediting. Use only when necessary.
- *Limit "following credits":* Do not have sales credits "follow" sales personnel to new territories or job assignments. Buy out any credit rather than use tracking of actual credits.

SUMMARY

Policies, procedures and accountabilities, automation, and reporting are key components of the overall administrative support for effective sales compensation programs. These administrative systems require substantial investment. While not highly visible to sales personnel when functioning correctly, they become very visible (and distracting) when not operating effectively.

Chapter 12

Implementation and Communication

All sales compensation plans should have a published effective start date and a termination date. The effective period of the compensation program should match the company's fiscal year. The termination of the sales compensation program on an annual basis gives sales management the opportunity to redirect sales force efforts to better serve changing corporate objectives. The anticipated announcement of the new program, with new performance measures, goals, and payout formula, provides sales management with an eager audience. Sales personnel want to learn how to excel under the new pay program. Sales management should fully optimize this leadership opportunity.

The successful launch of a new sales compensation program requires the combination of exceptional program implementation and inspired communication.

IMPLEMENTATION

While the communication about the new pay plan occurs close to the effective start date, implementation efforts begin much earlier. Depending on the scope of changes and the size of the sales force, implementation activities could begin months prior to the effective date of the new pay program.

Implementation Checklist

The following provides a checklist of implementation actions:

- *Program approval and funding:* Before proceeding with implementation actions, obtain program approval from the senior management team. Depending on internal practices, this process may be informal and cursory or require extensive documentation and final signature concurrence. Senior management needs to approve both program design and all costs including payout and administrative costs. An approval package should contain the following information:
  - New fiscal year sales objectives and goals
  - Assessment of current program
  - Major revisions with comparison of the new plan to the old plan
  - A spreadsheet of all plans with target total compensation, mix, leverage, performance measures, weighting of performance measures, payment periods, and key crediting rules
- *Support programs:* All issues regarding quota management including quota allocation, account assignments, and sales crediting need final resolution prior to program implementation.
- *Automation systems:* Test all automation systems—data input, transaction processing, and output reporting. Conduct several mock runs to fully test the automation program. Provide full testing up to and including payroll file production.
- *Procedures:* Have fully documented administrative procedures with workflow charts, steps, and assigned accountabilities.

Conversion and Transition Methods

Conversion and transition methods provide the means to move from an old plan to a new plan. The extent of the changes is a function of the degree of program change in one or more of the following plan elements:

- *Total target cash compensation (TTCC):* The company may need to increase or decrease TTCC. Increases to total target cash compensation amounts are easy to implement, but reductions are not.

- *Pay mix:* The pay mix may need to change due to changes in eligibility, sales role influence, or labor market practices. When management reduces the size of the target incentive, management must increase base salary, often at amounts outside normal base pay changes. However, when management increases the incentive component (without changing the total target cash compensation), management must reduce the base pay portion.

- *Performance measures:* Changing performance measures will require a change in selling activities and focus. In some cases, sales representatives can quickly make the necessary changes. Other types of performance changes may take several months as sales personnel become more proficient (and customers more accepting) of new selling messages.

- *Payment periods:* A change in performance period may affect income cash flow payout to sales personnel. A certain adjustment period may be necessary to accommodate a different payout schedule.

Minor changes to the pay program may require no conversion or transition support. However, major changes—those causing significant pay dislocations—between the old plan and the new plan may require one or more of the following techniques:

- *Cold cut:* A cold-cut approach provides no transition support. If a major change benefits sales personnel, such as giving them a higher base salary with no incentive reduction, then an immediate change is welcomed by all. However, if the change presents significantly new challenges to earn compensation, then a cold cut might be a major burden on sales personnel. The company may face the risk of excessive turnover. However, some management teams use this drastic management intervention to separate those who wish to continue with the company from those who seek their futures elsewhere.

- *Guarantees:* When pay dislocations are significant, sales management might consider providing guarantee payments:

  - *Flat amount:* The easiest is to offer a flat guarantee during a defined transition period with no downside or upside opportunity.

  - *Guarantee with upside:* A favorable guarantee type for sales personnel is to provide upside earnings for sales performance that exceeds the guarantee level.

  - *Declining guarantee:* Another guarantee type is to provide a graduated declining guarantee where the amount of the guarantee is reduced each month until it expires.

  - *Two-check method:* Sales organizations that need to introduce an at-risk program often use the two-check guarantee method. With this approach the payroll department splits the current paycheck into two separate checks: the first represents the new base salary and the second check represents the new, at-risk incentive element. Management informs the participants that the second check will become variable after the guarantee period expires.

  - *Grandfathering:* If the new pay program calls for reducing pay levels, another approach is to grandfather highly paid participants without reducing target pay levels for either base salary or incentive pay.

CONVERSION METHODS: BEST PRACTICES

When converting to a new sales compensation program, sales management will find many competing objectives including achieving sales objectives, controlling costs, and not demoralizing or upsetting the sales force. However, a few principles can help reconcile some of these conflicting issues. First, the role of the sales compensation program is to drive sales efforts to meet company objectives. Sales management should avoid conversion techniques that unnecessarily delay this intent such as long guarantee periods and grandfathering. Second, buy out any commitment such as carryover credits from previous sales that will distract sales personnel from their current assignments. Lastly, don't delay the inevitable. Accept the fact that not all changes will be popular.

Rollout Schedule

Prepare a rollout schedule including steps and accountabilities for implementation of the sales compensation program. Prepare a comprehensive outline of who, what, when, and where for the roll-out of the new sales compensation program. Of course, the larger the sales organization, the more complex the rollout effort and thus the need for a more extensive and complete rollout documentation.

COMMUNICATION

At its heart, sales compensation is a communication device: It tells salespeople what's important and what's not important. Day after day, the sales compensation program reiterates what management seeks. Sales management wants the sales force to understand the plan, support it, and strive to meet its objectives. The purpose of a well-designed communication effort is to increase sales force commitment to the sales compensation program and its strategic objectives.

An effective communication effort is made up of eight components:

- Communication schedule
- Sales leadership message
- Program launch material
- Field management training
- Sales force communication
- Plan documentation
- Performance and payout reporting
- Plan updates and advisory notes

Communication Schedule

Each company will have its own unique time line for its sales compensation communication effort. Start by identifying the most important date—the announcement to the sales force—and work backward. While effective communication theory recommends making the announcement prior to the plan effective date, most sales executives prefer to announce the new program after the old program has expired so as not to distract sales personnel during the final weeks of the fiscal year. For example, for fiscal years ending December 31, the new sales compensation program will become effective January 1. Plan the roll-out of the new sales compensation program to occur *after* January 1, and as late as the second or third week of January.

Sales Leadership Message

The launch of the new sales compensation program gives the sales executive a superb platform to articulate the sales objectives for the coming year and inspire commitment to sales results.

The more personalized the delivery, the more effective the message. Face-to-face communication is better than a live video broadcast; a live video broadcast is better than a DVD/VHS video presentation; a DVD/VHS video presentation is better than a nonvideo Web-cast presentation; and a Web-cast presentation is better than a memo.

Figure 12-1 is an example of the tenor of an effective sales leadership message.

A message from the VP of Sales—Your New Sales Compensation Program

I am pleased to announce the new sales compensation program for this coming year! Your manager will be giving you detailed information on how the program works and how it will affect your earning opportunities.

The strength of our company is tied directly to the success of our salespeople. Our customers and our competitors recognize our sales force as a critical competitive element of our success. Without our skilled, motivated, and high-caliber sales personnel, we would not have the success we have today.

However, we cannot live on our past success. We need to be ready and committed to meeting new and demanding sales objectives. These objectives will change from year to year and we must change, too.

A key element to our sales effectiveness is our sales compensation program. Each year we reexamine our pay program to ensure it provides competitive pay opportunities for you and supports our critical sales strategies.

For this coming fiscal year, we need to maintain focus on revenue growth, but with greater attention to profitable revenue growth. In addition to ensuring our pay levels are competitive, we have made adjustments to reward those who achieve profitable sales. If you are a direct seller, you will find a new measure in your pay plan: "price realization." The idea is simple—sell higher volumes and avoid deep discounting to earn exceptional pay.

We are committed to making you successful by providing you with the tools you need to do your job. The new sales compensation plan represents one such solution. We join with you to make this a successful year for the company and for you personally.

Good Selling!

Figure 12-1 Effective sales leadership message.

Program Launch Material

Depending on the extent of change and the size of the sales organization, the prepared communication material will vary. Use the following as a checklist for material preparation:

- Sales leadership message
- Field manager communication training material
- Plan documentation
- E-mail announcement
- Web site update
- Employee announcement packet
- Field manager presentation material

Field Management Training

Field managers should present the new sales compensation program to sales personnel. Investment in field manager training provides exponential return on the program effectiveness. Bring region and district managers together for a full-day training program. Devote the first half of the day to plan explanation. For the second half of the day, have the field managers practice their communication presentations.

Sales Force Communication

As with any promotion, multiple communication events from different sources who restate and support the primary theme create focus, understanding, and retention. The following communications events help promote the sales compensation program to the sales personnel:

- *Sales leadership message:* As mentioned before, the sales leadership message provides the foundation for all subsequent sales compensation messages. Ideally this message would be delivered at the national sales meeting, in person, to all sales personnel.

- *Field manager plan introduction:* Regional and district managers should introduce the new sales compensation program to their field personnel.
- *Sales supervisor coaching:* In one-on-one sessions, the sales supervisor meets with each sales representative to discuss how the new sales compensation program will affect the salesperson's income. Advice on how to sell effectively to optimize the sales incentive plan will provide the right direction to sales personnel.
- *Web site content:* Most sales organizations now have a sales department portal for all content information related to selling efforts. Devote a section of this sales department portal to sales compensation documentation including plan description, sales leadership messages, Q&A, and policies and procedures. Also, provide a formula calculator to test the payout potential of the program.
- *Questions and answers (Q&As):* Prepare the expected Q&As that will most likely arise as part of the sales compensation program implementation. See Figure 12-2 for an example.

Plan Documentation

Prepare a complete sales compensation plan document for each plan. Include the following sections in the plan document:

1. *Introduction and strategic objective.* The opening section provides an overview of the strategic objectives for the sales job and how the sales compensation program supports these goals.
2. *Compensation philosophy.* A brief statement provides an overview of the company's competitive position and role of incentive compensation.
3. *Plan overview.* The plan overview section provides an overview of the plan components and their intent.

New Sales Compensation Program
Questions and Answers

Why are we changing the sales compensation plan? The old one was working great.

We need to continue to focus on the company's business objectives. Our focus is on profitable revenue growth. We want you to share in the results of increasing our profits by negotiating better pricing.

Will my incentive pay be reduced?

We are not reducing the target incentive opportunity. In fact, we are increasing next year's earning potential. However, you must succeed within the definition of the new sales compensation plan. So you may make more money, or less, depending on how you perform under the new program.

Why is the new plan more complex than the old plan?

While it does, at first glance, seem more complex, it is really simple. The major change is a new measure on profitability.

I have noticed that the threshold has been raised from 70% to 85%. Why the change?

We are moving to a more performance-based pay plan. In the past, almost every sales-person reached the threshold. Now, we want to give the threshold meaning. If you are not achieving at least 85% of you goal, then we need to review how we can help you to succeed.

How does our incentive plan stack up with others in our industry?

Our HR department tracks our competitive pay position very carefully. It participates in industry surveys of pay practices. Our objective is to provide outstanding pay for outstanding performance, average pay for average performance, and low pay for low performance. While each company's formula may differ, our actual pay levels are very consistent with our objectives.

Will timing of payouts be different?

No, you will continue to earn your volume incentive monthly and your strategic objective performance quarterly.

How will I know what my payout will be?

We have a new Web site (www.salesourcompany.com) that allows you to review your performance statement in real time. The site also provides an estimate of how much you will earn if your performance continues with its current trend.

Figure 12-2 Questions and answers.

4. *Plan elements.* This section explains each element of the compensation plan, for example, base salary, volume incentive, and strategic bonus.
5. *Program policies.* Describe applicable territory configuration, quota management, and sales crediting policies in this section.
6. *Formula calculation example.* Provide one or more formula calculation examples showing how the pay plan functions.
7. *Employment status policies.* This section outlines how employment status (transfers, promotions, terminations, retirement, and death) affect the incentive plan.
8. *Rights and obligations.* Legal rights and obligations presented in this section include plan governance and exceptions.
9. *Glossary.* Provide a glossary of terms for easy plan interpretation.

See Appendix A for an example of a sales compensation plan document. Have sales personnel sign the performance plan summary that describes their territory, quota, and target incentive amount.

For paperless confirmation, have the salesperson click on a box on the Web site to confirm that he or she has read and understands the sales compensation plan. Make no payments until this electronic acceptance is obtained.

Performance and Payout Reporting

To provide the real-time reinforcement of the incentive plan, provide comprehensive and timely reports on sales performance and payouts. Sales personnel should be able to see all transactions, adjustments, credits, and payout amounts with relative ease. Drill-down Web sites are ideal for providing this level of always-ready detail. Add informative motivational features to the reports by displaying the performance and pay information in charts that show progress year-to-date, year-over-year, and individual progress as compared to the salesperson's peer group. Provide other interested parties with program reports on a regular basis.

Plan Updates and Advisory Notes

Provide a means to issue plan updates and advisory notes regarding plan interpretation. Use a memo format for non-Web-based plan communication. Have multiple approval signatures. Designate a central repository for these updates, changes, and advisory notes.

No Change This Year?

What if your company requires no change? The strategy, job content, and performance measures have not changed. What should you do? Don't miss the opportunity to use the annual review of the plan to restate and support the ongoing strategy. A new plan year still provides the same opportunity to reach out and communicate with sales personnel.

SUMMARY

Implementation and communication activate the sales compensation program. Carefully plan the implementation steps. Leave nothing to chance. Confirm accountabilities, test and retest system solutions, and monitor progress.

Think of the communication program not as an administrative event, but as an advertising and/or marketing event. Make use of the creative talents within your company to develop a theme to market the new sales compensation program to the sales force. Make sure all levels of sales management participate in the process. Use personal communication whenever possible. Your actions will tell the sales force how to act—if you think it's important, they will think it's important. If you don't think it's important—and you suboptimize your communication opportunity—your salespeople won't think it's important either.

Chapter 13

Program Assessment

How effective is the sales compensation program? It's a simple question and is often asked by senior management. The company expends significant amounts of money on the sales force, especially on the compensation paid to sales personnel.

But is it working? Is the company getting the right sales force focus? Is the sales force motivated by the pay program?

Use the following five factors to assess the sales compensation program:

- *Strategic alignment:* How well does the plan support the company's business objectives?
- *Employee motivation:* Do the sales personnel strive to earn incentive pay by excelling on the program performance measures?
- *Best-practice variance:* While some companies will intentionally vary from best practices, knowing these variances may help identify unexpected consequences.
- *Return on investment:* Is the company getting an effective return on investment?
- *Program management:* Is the program management consistent with plan documentation? Is it timely? Accurate?

Each year, sales management should undertake a full, formal review of all five of these factors. For sales organizations facing volatile market conditions, more frequent assessments may be necessary.

STRATEGIC ALIGNMENT

The sales compensation program needs to support the company's business objectives. An assessment of the sales compensation program begins with a review of how well the compensation program supports the strategic objectives of the company.

Begin with a confirmation of the company's objectives. Gather any written statements of financial, product, and customer goals, and then proceed with senior management interviews. These interviews will provide contemporary confirmation of the goals of the company. Include both the vice president level and other headquarters personnel interviews including finance, product management, marketing, and sales leadership. Prepare a summary statement of sales objectives for review and confirmation by senior management.

Next, review all the performance measures in the sales compensation program to assess how each measure contributes to achieving the company's objectives. Examine the importance of each measure by reviewing the relative weighting of the measures.

Finally, examine the performance payout information by performance measure to see the relationship between compensation and performance.

Figure 13-1 displays the relationship between total pay and sales volume. The relationship is moderate. This would suggest further investigation to examine how incentive pay relates to quota performance.

As we can see in Figure 13-2, when compared to quota performance, incentive pay is more closely correlated, which means that the pay system provides greater incentive rewards as sales volume quota performance improves.

Figure 13-1 Pay versus volume performance.

A similar analysis can be done with gross margin performance. In Figure 13-3 on page 234, total compensation is compared to gross margin performance.

Examine the relationship between pay and performance using a variety of dispersion charts to review trends and pay and performance relationships. Prepare unique charts for each job. Be careful to eliminate data of personnel who only worked part of the year.

Using the dispersion charts, determine what the program really rewards versus what it purports to reward.

Going out of business, slowly. Unknown to management, the incentive plan of a large regional chain of coffee/doughnut shops was putting the company out of business. In an effort to improve profits, the new financially centric management team

Figure 13-2 Incentive pay versus quota performance.

Figure 13-3 Pay versus profit.

introduced an incentive plan to reduce baking waste. Because each store baked its own fresh product, the new incentive plan was designed to discourage excess production. Store managers in an attempt to lower the waste rate produced fewer doughnuts than were needed. This had a subtle yet negative impact on customer service. As the years passed, the cycle of low production led to declining customer traffic, which led to further reduction in production, which led to further reduction in customer traffic, and so on.

Preferred Solution: Revamp the whole market concept. Introduce new products, push sales with a new marketing campaign, and provide a new pay system to reward revenue growth.

EMPLOYEE MOTIVATION

Collect additional information on sales personnel motivation. Conduct field interviews and focus group interviews to learn what features of the incentive program are effective. Gather survey responses using Web-based surveys. Ask questions about the following items:

- *Plan effectiveness:* Total compensation, target incentive pay, program focus

- *Communication:* Understanding of the plan
- *Administration:* Payments, issue resolution
- *Quotas:* Allocation process, fairness
- *Sales crediting:* Rules, consistency
- *Recognition plan:* Impact
- *Contests:* Effectiveness

Sales management should also ask sales personnel this very simple question: Does the sales compensation program motivate you to achieve the company's objectives?

Finally, examine both new hire acceptances and voluntary termination rates. Determine why applicants decline offers. Use a telephone follow-up or a questionnaire. Be specific; ask if the pay program is competitive. Analyze turnover rates to ensure that high-performing personnel are staying and low-performing personnel are departing.

BEST-PRACTICE VARIANCE

Well-designed sales compensation programs share similar design characteristics. Use the following list to review each sales compensation plan:

- *Eligibility:* Eligibility for sales compensation should be reserved for those jobs where the incumbents (1) have customer contact, (2) persuade the customer to act, and (3) contribute to the revenue production of the company.
- *Mix:* Pay mix, the split of total target cash compensation (TTCC) between target base salary and target incentive, should reflect the degree of influence of the job. Where sales personnel have high influence over the customer's decision to buy, provide a low base salary and a high incentive opportunity. Where sales personnel represent only one factor affecting the buyer's

decision, provide a high base salary component while keeping the target incentive component smaller.

- *Leverage:* As confirmed by market data, ensure that the best performers—the 90th percentile of job incumbents—earn three times the target incentive amount for outstanding performance. Avoid caps on the sales compensation plan.

- *Performance measures and weights:* Always have a revenue production measure to drive sales volume performance. Restrict the number of measures to three or fewer. Weight the measures to reflect importance of the measures.

- *Quotas distribution:* The target is for two-thirds of sales personnel to reach and exceed quota and one-third not to reach quota. There should be no bias in the quota allocation process. As Figure 13-4 illustrates, the size of territories should not have a positive or negative influence on the quota performance.

- *Performance and payment periods:* Match the payment period to the performance period. Use cumulative-to-date payments when payouts occur more frequently than the performance period.

- *Formula type:* Use a target incentive commission formula when territories are equal; use a target incentive bonus formula when revenue levels among territories are significantly dissimilar.

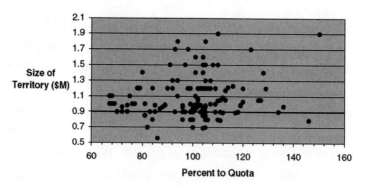

Figure 13-4 Quota fairness.

- *Market data:* Set pay levels consistent with market pay data. Participate in market surveys conducted by a third party featuring uniform data submission standards, mandatory job matching sessions, and incumbent-based data collection and reporting. Purchase surveys annually. Ensure to have more than one survey source for each benchmark job.

RETURN ON INVESTMENT

Sales management can monitor the cost of the sales force, specifically the sales compensation program (see Figure 13-5). Regular trend analysis provides a means to track return on sales expense.

PROGRAM MANAGEMENT

Evaluation of program management includes the following:

- *Conformity to plan design:* How well does the application of the incentive plan match the plan documentation?
- *Accuracy of payments:* How accurate are payout calculations? What is the error and/or correction rate?

Figure 13-5 Sales costs.

- *Timeliness of payments:* Are payout checks issued at the stated time?
- *Resolution of exceptions:* How quickly do exceptions take to resolve?
- *Scope of reporting:* How extensive is the reporting of the sales compensation program to meet the needs of headquarters management, field sales management, and individual sales representatives?
- *Cost of administration:* How costly is it to administer the sales compensation program?
- *Annual audit:* How did the sales compensation program fare under the annual audit of the program conducted by the finance department?

Common Sales Compensation Symptoms

Here are several examples of common sales compensation symptoms:

1. *Unmotivated and frustrated sales personnel.* Something is wrong when sales personnel are unmotivated and frustrated. Careful examination of the incentive plan will determine if poor design features of the sales compensation program are contributing to this negative situation.
2. *Unpredictable over- or underpayments.* The pay plan should not hold "surprises" for either the sales personnel or sales management. Unexpected drops in income or excessive earnings means the sales compensation plan most likely has design errors.
3. *Excessive double crediting.* The sales compensation program should not rely on excessive double or split crediting to function correctly. Examine job design and sales crediting practices when horizontal sales credit exceeds real sales revenue by more than 115 percent.

SUMMARY

An assessment of the sales compensation program requires a multifactor review: strategic alignment, employee motivation, best-practice variance, return on investment, and program management. Some companies use a standing sales compensation review committee to monitor program effectiveness. Other companies make it a periodic project. Regardless, a comprehensive review of the sales compensation program should occur on an annual basis.

Chapter 14

Sales Compensation Design

Sales management should plan well in advance for a full redesign of the sales compensation program. Sales compensation redesign is an iterative process. For large sales organizations, this process could take up to 4 to 5 months elapse time. Smaller sales organizations, with 10 to 50 sales representatives with 3 or fewer sales jobs should start their redesign efforts at least 2 months in advance of the implementation date. Sales organizations with fewer than 10 sales personnel should give themselves at least a month elapse time for sales compensation design efforts.

WHY IS "TWEAKING" BAD?

Making minor adjustments to the sales compensation program on an annual basis is an acceptable and preferred practice when underlying influencing factors have changed very little. However, be wary of the practice of tweaking the sales compensation program. What is the difference between minor adjustments and tweaking? Minor adjustments assume that sales management has made a complete review of all the plans and the limited changes fit within the context of the overall program design. Tweaking, however, makes isolated changes and patches to the pay program outside the context of the overall design. While such changes often reflect good intentions, the summation of these tweaks can create confusing and convoluted sales compensation plans.

THE SALES COMPENSATION DESIGN PROCESS

An important element of the sales compensation design process is the involvement and participation of key stakeholders. As the design steps presented below suggest, various points within the design process require collaborative decision-making. These involvement steps are needed to help resolve competing objectives and make tough resource allocation decisions. For example, when selecting performance measures, the senior management team needs concurrence on the use of the right measures to ensure alignment with the company's objectives. Unfortunately, sales, finance, operations, and marketing may have different and competing expectations for the sales force. Leaders of these departments need to meet to identify key measures for inclusion in (or exclusion from) the sales compensation program. Likewise, similar collaborative decision-making is necessary when providing automation provisioning for the sales compensation program. Sales operations, finance, and information technology (IT) need to review various choices affecting functionality and costs.

This collaborative approach is a vote against the expert-recommended solution. Whether concocted by an inside resource, the vice president of sales, or an outside consultant, such expert solutions are often counterproductive. There is no right answer to sales compensation design. The right answer is a shared judgment by the leadership team. The leadership team needs to "work the issue" to examine implications and impacts of various alternatives as they attempt to drive company objectives.

TEN STEPS TO SALES COMPENSATION DESIGN

Regardless of the size of the organization and the elapse time devoted to the redesign effort, the following 10 steps provide a road map for all sales organizations. Each step provides a crucial element to ensure successful redesign. This process should be repeated every year.

Step 1: Fact Finding

The first step is to gather information about the current program and confirm the company's business objectives. Undertake the following actions to prepare a *Fact Finding Report:*

- *Interview senior management:* Gather perspectives regarding the current program and information about future sales objectives from senior management.
- *Interview headquarters staff:* Learn what is working with the current pay program and where improvements are needed. Gather all written documentation regarding the current and proposed jobs and organization structure. Collect all information about the current pay programs including policies and practices related to account assignment, quota allocation, and sales crediting.
- *Interview field sales management:* Collect field perspectives regarding the effectiveness of the current program. Capture any suggestions for changes.
- *Interview sales personnel:* Learn how sales personnel view the current sales compensation program. Assess their understanding of the current plan. Gain their views on how to improve the program. Document job content. Ask sales personnel to confirm how the current sales compensation program supports the charter of their sales job. For large sales forces, gather electronic

survey responses on the effectiveness of the sales compensation program.

- *Purchase external survey data:* Obtain competitive market data from sales compensation survey sources. (See Appendix B for a partial listing.)
- *Assemble pay and performance data:* Gather quantitative information on the current program—pay and performance data.
- *Obtain strategic goals:* Solicit internal documentation on the forthcoming strategic goals of the company.
- *Document mid-year changes:* Gather all mid-year changes including program design, account assignment changes, quota changes, and sales personnel movement.

Step 2: Assessment

Conduct analytical and comparative assessment analysis. Conduct the following analysis for inclusion in the *Assessment Report.*

- *Make competitive market comparison:* Compare actual pay levels with labor market practices.
- *Examine pay and performance relationship:* Prepare dispersion charts showing the relationship between performance and incentive payouts.
- *Test quota system:* Examine the quota system for proper balance of performance below and above quota. Ensure the program is free of unintended bias.
- *Review performance measures:* Determine if performance measures support the company's business objectives.
- *Calculate return on investment:* Prepare trend charts showing the change in cost of sales and return on investment.
- *Audit support programs:* Review support programs to ensure compliance with policies for account assignment, quota allocation, and sales crediting.

Step 3: Alignment

The alignment step provides senior management with its first collaborative involvement in the design process. During this step of the project, senior management reviews a summary of the *Fact Finding Report* and *Assessment Report* prepared for Steps 1 and 2, respectively. Then working as a group, the senior team including the general manager, top sales executive, top finance executive, top marketing executive, and head of human resources will confirm the *Sales Alignment Statement,* which includes:

- *Corporate sales strategy:* Specify the strategic role of the sales force regarding revenue, profit, product, and customer strategies.
- *Sales compensation principles:* Examine sales compensation design principles regarding eligibility, total target cash compensation (TTCC), mix, leverage, performance measures, quota allocation, and pay and performance periods for appropriateness. Update the sales compensation principles as appropriate.

Step 4: Program Design

For Step 4, assemble a design task force consisting of sales management, marketing, finance, and human resources to examine design alternatives and select a preferred design. For small organizations, the design task force will most likely be those who authored the *Sales Alignment Statement.* Larger sales organizations might appoint specialists from each department to serve on the task force. Companies that have multiple sales entities should assemble a design task force for each sales unit. The task force develops preferred sales compensation designs during the following meetings:

- *Meeting 1: Review of current documentation.* Present and discuss all relevant material: *Fact Finding Report, Assessment Report,*

Job Title	Eligible	TTCC	Mix	Leverage	Measures	Weighting	Formula Type
Worldwide Sales Executive	Yes	$250K	80/20	3x	Volume	75%	Bonus
					Profit	25%	Bonus
Senior Sales Representative	Yes	$150K	75/25	3x	Volume	50%	Bonus
					Retention	50%	Bonus
Territory Representative	Yes	$ 75K	60/40	3x	Volume	75%	Commission
					New Accounts	25%	Bonus
Telephone Sales	Yes	$ 65K	↓	↓	↓	↓	↓
Product Overlay	Yes	↓	↓	↓	↓	↓	↓

Figure 14-1. Sales Compensation Design Elements.

and *Sales Alignment Statement.* If participants are new to the design of sales compensation, provide an overview of key sales compensation concepts.

- *Meetings 2 and 3: Design sales compensation plans.* Work through the sales compensation design for each job. Design by element, not by job. Use Figure 14-1, an example of a spreadsheet, to record design decisions.

- *Meeting 4: Confirm preferred designs.* Review proposed sales compensation designs. Make necessary adjustments.

Step 5: Support Programs

A team of sales management personnel prepares guidelines for the territory configuration, quota management, account assignment, and sales crediting rules. Develop estimates of territory loading, quota allocation numbers, and the impact of various sales crediting practices. Prepare a *Support Program Impact Report.*

Step 6: Modeling and Costing

The sales operations function examines cost by modeling the overall program costs and preparing individual income estimates.

Provide these to senior management for approval in a *Program Cost Report*.

Step 7: Automation

Assemble a work team of specialists from sales operations, finance, and information technology (IT) to examine automation alternatives and select a preferred system. Get approval and funding for a solution. (See Appendix C for a list of incentive software vendors.) Test automation solution prior to program launch.

Step 8: Implementation

Prepare an implementation schedule for program roll-out, conversion, communication, and systems support. Allocate responsibilities to assigned personnel for each component of the implementation effort.

Step 9: Communication

Prepare communication collateral, train field managers, and populate Web site with relevant content.

Step 10: Administration

Prepare administrative procedures and practices. Communicate accountabilities and time commitments to responsible personnel.

Ten Steps—Work Plan

Prepare a work plan (see Figure 14-2) *to track progress* of the sales compensation redesign effort.

Project Steps	1	2	3	4	5	6	7	8	9	10	11	12	13	14	15	16	17
1. Fact Finding	X																
2. Assessment		X	X														
3. Alignment				X	X												
4. Program Design					X	X											
5. Support Programs						X	X	X	X								
6. Modeling and Costing									X	X	X						
7. Automation											X	X	X	X	X	X	
8. Implementation												X	X	X	X	X	
9. Communication														X	X	X	
10. Administration																X	X

Figure 14-2 Sales compensation work plan—weeks.

SUMMARY

The sales compensation design process requires a dedicated effort. Appoint a process leader to facilitate the design process. Ensure you have adequate time to accomplish each of the design steps. Conduct the process each year. Follow these 10 steps to keep the compensation plans contemporary with current sales strategies.

Closing Notes

Sales compensation provides sales management with a powerful tool to help focus sales personnel efforts. However, as we have learned, building an effective sales compensation plan is not a casual task. Following the approach and concepts presented in this book, you will find the task accomplishable. Here are some summary notes as you undertake your sales compensation design efforts.

- *Sales compensation works:* While not appropriate for all selling jobs, sales compensation provides the means to reward superior sales results. Sales personnel respond to the opportunity to perform well.
- *Sales compensation is one of many types of incentive compensation plans:* Sales compensation plans feature a substantial upside opportunity for placing part of the target compensation at risk. Other pay plans such as gainsharing, add-on, and management bonus plans serve different and worthy purposes.
- *Income producers and sales representatives are paid differently:* Income producers earn a portion of their sales production. Sales representatives earn a percent of target incentive—less than target incentive for below-expected performance, more than target incentive for above-expected performance.

- *Sales compensation follows job design:* Sales compensation plans support sales job design. Changes in strategy and focus will change the sales job. If the sales job changes, so must the sales compensation plan.
- *Sales compensation administration requires resources:* Whether as head count or automation support, the sales compensation program requires company resources for ongoing success.
- *Collaborative design process promotes the best solution:* Involving key decision makers in the design process will significantly improve the outcome of the design process.
- *Communicate, communicate, and communicate:* Use every means to communicate the new plan to participants.

With the right investment of time in the right design process, you can capitalize on the driven enthusiasm of sales personnel earning outstanding pay for exceeding company objectives!

Illustrative Sales Compensation Plan

Utility Energy, Inc.
Sales Compensation Plan
Sales Representatives
for Plan Year
20XX

CONTENTS

INTRODUCTION

This document presents the Sales Compensation Plan (for Sales Representatives) for Utility Energy, Inc.

Your compensation plan rewards incremental increases in sales performance with incremental increases in compensation earnings.

As you improve your sales performance, you will have the opportunity to achieve outstanding earnings.

SECTION 1: PLAN OVERVIEW

Why Do We Need a Compensation Plan?

The immediate success of Utility Energy, Inc., depends on our ability to rapidly penetrate mid-level business customers outside our traditional service area. To meet these objectives, our compensation plan will provide the following:

- Unique compensation solutions that match plan designs with job responsibilities and desired behaviors
- Focused plan elements that drive achievement of business objectives and selling strategy
- Significant rewards for high achievers

Compensation Philosophy

In general, this plan is intended to communicate a compensation philosophy consistent with the following points:

- *Strategic:* The plan designs will support, drive, and encourage vision and overall business strategy achievement of Utility Energy, Inc. Our goal is to target mid-level customers.
- *Competitive:* The Sales Compensation Plan is designed to attract and retain top performers. We will reward outstanding performance with exceptional earnings opportunities.
- *Fair:* We will develop compensation policies that reward individual achievement in support of sales goals.
- *Simple:* We have designed the new plan to ensure that the mechanics and policies are easy to understand and communicate.

Competitive Earnings

We are committed to the success of Utility Energy, Inc. We provide competitive earnings to those of you who can help us attain our goals. Those who consistently sell at the highest levels of volume will earn the highest levels of compensation.

SECTION 2: 20XX SALES COMPENSATION PLAN COMPONENTS

The 20XX Compensation Plan consists of two components: Base Salary and MWH (megawatts per hour) units commission based on achievement of unit sales and number of contracts completed.

Base Salary

All individuals covered under the new compensation plan will receive a base salary. The base salary is managed within a pay range. Merit increases are provided on an annual basis consistent with the company's salary merit increase guidelines.

MWH Units and Number of Contracts Commission

The MWH Units and Number of Contracts Commission are based on the number of megawatt hours sold and number of

Table A-1 Commission Rate per MWH

Contracts	MWH 80,000–120,000	MWH >120,000
10–19	.08	.09
20–29	.18	.20
30–39	.29	.31
40–49	.31	.37
50+	.33	.44

Table A-2 Guaranteed Incentive Table

Quarter	Percent Target Earnings Guaranteed	Payout Amount Guaranteed	Cumulative Payout Guaranteed
1	100%	$8,750.00	$ 8,750.00
2	75%	$6,562.50	$15,312.50
3	50%	$4,375.00	$19,687.50
4	25%	$2,187.00	$21,875.00

contracts completed at the individual level. Payout will begin once MWH unit sales are equal to or exceed 80,000 and the number of contracts is equal to or exceeds 10. For example, performance of 80% of target (96,000 MWHs and 24 contracts) will yield 50% of target payout ($17,280). Performance at target (120,000 MWHs and 30 contracts) will yield 100% of the target payout ($34,800). Performance above the target level will receive an accelerated commission payout. For example, performance of 120% of target (144,000 MWHs and 36 contracts) will yield 130% of the target payout ($44,640). See Table A-1.

Note that a minimum incentive of $21,875 will be guaranteed for the first year of the plan (20XX). This represents 100% of quarter 1, 75% of quarter 2, 50% of quarter 3, and 25% of quarter 4 target earnings. See Table A-2.

SECTION 3: 20XX SALES COMPENSATION PLAN POLICIES AND DEFINITIONS

Purpose

The purpose of the Utility Energy, Inc., Compensation Program (the "Program") is to reward Participants for identifying and growing business with new customers.

Definitions

The following terms shall have the following meanings for the purposes of the Program:

- *Award:* The payment of dollars to a Participant as determined by this Program.
- *Company:* Utility Energy, Inc.
- *Disability:* Total disability as defined in the Company's long-term disability plan in effect at the time of disability.
- *Participant:* Any employee of the Company who is selected to participate in the Program.
- *Threshold:* In order to receive an incentive payout, it is a requirement for all Participants of this Program to exceed a minimum accomplishment of plan.
- *Incentive Payout:* For all Participants, incentive will accumulate from dollar one, but will not be paid until the thresholds for all measures have been exceeded.
- *Large Orders Rule:* If an order is received that exceeds 12,000 MWH, you will only be credited for 12,000. Exceptions to this rule must have approval by the Sales Director and Managing Director prior to the booking of the order.
- *Program:* Utility Energy, Inc., Compensation Program as originally adopted or, if amended or supplemented, as amended or supplemented.

Award Value Determination

Participants will begin earning incentive once their minimum thresholds have been exceeded.

"Incentive Payout" will be paid quarterly once thresholds are achieved.

Conventional rounding rules apply: >.5 round up, <.5 round down.

"Large Orders Rule" will be used to limit credit for orders in excess of order size boundary of 12,000 MWH.

Payments

Eligibility to Participate: Participants must hold a job in one of the participating categories for a minimum of 30 consecutive days in the calendar year in order to be eligible for an incentive payout. If you should leave Utility Energy, Inc., you will receive an incentive payment equivalent to that which you would have received for the last full quarter you worked.

Normal Case: Payments will be made quarterly, as soon as practical after the close of the quarter, but no later than ninety (90) days after the end of the quarter or year. Cumulative incentive earned to date will be calculated each quarter. The amount paid out each quarter will be the cumulative incentive earned to date less any payouts made in previous quarters.

Death, Disability, Retirement, or Termination (Voluntary/ Involuntary): If a Participant dies, becomes disabled, retires, or terminates within the meaning of the Program, he/she shall receive an Award for all bookings through the last full quarter of employment, and shall forfeit the Award for any uncompleted quarter.

Promotions/Transfers to Nonincentive Eligible Positions: If a Participant is promoted or transferred to a job in the Company that is not eligible for any incentive payment, he/she shall be entitled to a pro-rated payment of Awards for any period completed.

Promotions/Transfers to Incentive Eligible Positions: If a Participant is promoted or transferred to a job in the Company that is eligible for incentive, his/her total incentive payment will be prorated based on the amount of time spent in each position.

Partial Year Participation: The structure of the incentive plan is based upon a Participant's full year participation. We also recognize that people can enter the program at any time during the year. In those situations the following will apply:

- *Individual Contributors:* If an individual is eligible to become a Participant of the Program for a period of less than 12 months, a plan will be assigned based upon the months of eligibility remaining in the calendar year.

Deviations from these guidelines require written approval from the Sales Director and the Managing Director.

Crediting

Megawatt hours sold will be estimated based upon historical usage plus or minus adjustments according to usual company practices. Contracts will be credited when the contract is signed.

Cancellations and Deductions

Contracts canceled within 90 days of the date performance begins on the contract will result in sales being deducted from the representative's attainment.

Amendment and Termination

The Managing Director may terminate the Program at any time, treating any quarter then in effect as having ended as of the date he/she notifies the participants. The Managing Director may from time-to-time amend or revise the Program.

Effective Date

This Program shall become effective on January 1, 20XX.

Gender Plural and Singular

All pronouns and any variation thereof shall be deemed to refer to the masculine, feminine, or neuter as the identity of the person or persons may require. As the context may require the singular may be read as plural and the plural as singular.

Captions

The captions to the sections and paragraphs of the Program are for convenience only and shall not control or affect the meaning or construction of any of its provisions.

Management Judgment

In all cases, management reserves the right to reduce, modify, or withhold awards based upon individual performance or management modification in the Program. Such action requires the written approval of the Sales Director and Managing Director.

Table A-3 20XX Sales Compensation Plan and Calculation Examples

Example 1: *(Target Payout)*	Assume: Annual unit sales of 120,000 MWH and 30 contracts. Commission Rate: .29 (Look up rate on table.) Calculation: .29 × 120,000 MWH = $34,840
Example 2:	Assume: Annual unit sales of 96,000 MWH and 15 contracts. Commission Rate: .08 (Look up rate on table.) Calculation: .08 × 96,000 MWH = $7,680
Example 3:	Assume: Annual unit sales of 150,000 MWH and 50 contracts. Commission Rate: .44 (Look up rate on table.) Calculation: .44 × 150,000 MWH = $66,000

(Continued)

Table A-3 (*Continued*)

Example 4: *(Quarterly* *Payout* *Calculation* *Notes)*	Payouts begin when both MWH units and number of contracts are over threshold levels. If no commission is earned, a portion of the guaranteed amount will be paid out each quarter when thresholds are not reached. Payout for each quarter is the cumulative incentive earned to-date in the year, less previous payout amounts.
Assumptions:	Assume: • Q1 unit sales of 40,000 MWH, in 10 contracts • Q2 unit sales of 48,000 MWH, in 12 contracts • Q3 unit sales of 32,000 MWH, in 15 contracts • Q4 unit sales of 40,000 MWH, in 10 contracts

QUARTER 1 PAYOUT

Table A-4 Determining the Quarter 1 Payout

Step	Directions	Quarter 1 Calculation
Step 1: *Determine cumulative sales*	Add sales in all quarters to date.	Sales in all quarters to date are quarter 1 sales of 40,000 MWH.
Step 2: *Determine cumulative contracts*	Add contracts in all quarters to date.	Contracts in all quarters to date are quarter 1 contracts of 10.
Step 3: *Determine commission rate*	Look up cumulative sales and cumulative contracts performance in Table A-5 below to obtain commission rate.	Performance not on table because 40,000 is less than 80,000 MWH threshold. Hence, no commission rate applies, and no commission incentive is earned.
Step 4: *Calculate cumulative incentive earned to-date*	Multiply commission rate by cumulative number of MWHs.	Not applicable since no commission incentive earned.
Step 5: *Calculate guaranteed minimum incentive amount*	Look up cumulative payout guaranteed for quarter on guaranteed incentive table. If cumulative guaranteed payout is greater than incentive commission earned, then take as cumulative incentive earned.	Guaranteed minimum for quarter 1 is $8,750.
Step 6: *Calculate payout for quarter*	Subtract previous quarter earnings from cumulative incentive earned.	No previous quarters, so earnings are $8,750.

Table A-5 Commission Rate per MWH

Cumulative Contracts to Date	Cumulative MWH to Date	
	80,000–120,000	>120,000
10–19	.08	.09
20–29	.18	.20
30–39	.29	.31
40–49	.31	.37
50+	.33	.44

Quarter	Percent Target Earnings Guaranteed	Payout Amount Guaranteed	Cumulative Payout Guaranteed
1	100%	$8,750.00	$ 8,750.00
2	75%	$6,562.50	$15,312.50
3	50%	$4,375.00	$19,687.50
4	25%	$2,187.00	$21,875.00

Figure A-1 Guaranteed incentive chart.

QUARTER 2 PAYOUT

Table A-6 Determining the Quarter 2 Payout

Step	Directions	Quarter 2 Calculation
Step 1: *Determine cumulative sales*	Add sales in all quarters to date.	Quarter 1 + Quarter 2 MWHs = 40,000 + 48,000 = 88,000 MWHs
Step 2: *Determine cumulative contracts*	Add contracts in all quarters to date.	Quarter 1 + Quarter 2 Contracts = 10 + 12 = 22 Contracts
Step 3: *Determine commission rate*	Look up cumulative sales and cumulative contracts Figure A-7 to obtain commission rate.	88,000 is between 80,000 and 120,000 and 22 is between 20 and 29, hence commission rate is .18.
Step 4: *Calculate cumulative incentive earned to-date*	Multiply commission rate by cumulative number of MWHs.	Cumulative MWHs = 85,000. 88,000 × .18 = $15,840
Step 5: *Calculate guaranteed minimum incentive amount*	Look up cumulative payout guaranteed for quarter on guaranteed incentive table. If cumulative guaranteed payout is greater than incentive commission earned, then take as cumulative incentive earned.	Not applicable, since cumulative incentive, $15,840, is greater than $15,312.50.

(Continued)

Table A-6 *(Continued)*

Step 6: *Calculate payout for* *quarter*	Subtract previous quarter earnings from cumulative incentive earned.	Quarter 1 earnings are $8,750. Cumulative earnings are $15,840. $15,840 – $8,750 = $7,090. Quarter 2 payout = $7,090

Cumulative Contracts to Date	80,000–120,000	>120,000
10–19	.08	.09
20–29	.18	.20
30–39	.29	.31
40–49	.31	.37
50+	.33	.44

Figure A-2 Cumulative MWH to date.

Quarter	Percent Target Earnings Guaranteed	Payout Amount Guaranteed	Cumulative Payout Guaranteed
1	100%	$8,750.00	$ 8,750.00
2	75%	$6,562.50	$15,312.50
3	50%	$4,375.00	$19,687.50
4	25%	$2,187.00	$21,875.00

Figure A-3 Guaranteed incentive chart.

QUARTER 3 PAYOUT

Table A-7 Determining the Quarter 3 Payout

Step	Directions	Quarter 3 Calculation
Step 1: *Determine* *cumulative sales*	Add sales in all quarters to date.	40,000 + 48,000 + 32,000 = 120,000 MWHs
Step 2: *Determine* *cumulative contracts*	Add contracts in all quarters to date.	Quarter 1 + Quarter 2 Contracts = 10 + 12 + 15 = 37 Contracts
Step 3: *Determine* *commission rate*	Look up cumulative sales and cumulative contracts on table below to obtain commission rate.	120,000 is in the range 80,000 to 120,000 and 37 is between 30 and 39, hence commission rate is .29.
Step 4: *Calculate cumulative* *incentive earned* *to date*	Multiply commission rate by cumulative number of MWHs.	Cumulative MWHs = 120,000. 120,000 × .29 = $34,800

(Continued)

Table A-7 (Continued)

Step	Directions	Calculation
Step 5: *Calculate guaranteed minimum incentive amount*	Look up cumulative payout guaranteed for quarter on guaranteed incentive table. If cumulative guaranteed payout is greater than incentive commission earned, then take as cumulative incentive earned.	Not applicable, since cumulative incentive is greater than $19,687.50.
Step 6: *Calculate payout for quarter*	Subtract previous quarter earnings from cumulative incentive earned.	Quarter 1 earnings are $8,750. Quarter 2 earnings are $7,090. Cumulative earnings are $34,800. $34,800 – $7,090 – $8,750 = $18,160. Quarter 3 payout = $18,160

Cumulative Contracts To-Date	80,000–120,000	>120,000
10–19	.08	.09
20–29	.18	.20
30–39	.29	.31
40–49	.31	.37
50+	.33	.44

Figure A-4 Cumulative MWH to date.

Quarter	Percent Target Earnings Guaranteed	Payout Amount Guaranteed	Cumulative Payout Guaranteed
1	100%	$8,750.00	$ 8,750.00
2	75%	$6,562.50	$15,312.50
3	50%	$4,375.00	$19,687.50
4	25%	$2,187.00	$21,875.00

Figure A-5 Guaranteed incentive chart.

QUARTER 4 PAYOUT

Table A-8 Determining the Quarter 4 Payout

Step	Directions	Quarter 4 Calculation
Step 1: *Determine cumulative sales*	Add sales in all quarters to-date.	40,000 + 48,000 + 32,000 + 40,000 = 160,000 MWHs
Step 2: *Determine cumulative contracts*	Add contracts in all quarters to-date.	10 + 12 + 15 + 10 = 47 Contracts

(Continued)

Table A-8 (*Continued*)

Step	Directions	Quarter 4 Calculation
Step 3: *Determine commission rate*	Look up cumulative sales and cumulative contracts in Table A-9 to obtain commission rate.	160,000 is greater than 120,000 and 47 is between 40 and 49, hence commission rate is .37.
Step 4: *Calculate cumulative incentive earned to-date*	Multiply commission rate by cumulative number of MWHs.	Cumulative MWHs = 160,000. 160,000 × .37 = $59,200
Step 5: *Calculate guaranteed minimum incentive amount*	Look up cumulative payout guaranteed for quarter on guaranteed incentive table. If cumulative guaranteed payout is greater than incentive commission earned, then take as cumulative incentive earned.	Not applicable, since cumulative incentive of $59,200 is greater than $21,875.00.
Step 6: *Calculate payout for quarter*	Subtract previous quarter earnings from cumulative incentive earned.	Quarter 1 earnings are $8,750. Quarter 2 earnings are $7,090. Quarter 3 earnings are $18,160. Cumulative earnings are $59,200. $59,200 – $18,160 – $7,090 – $8,750 = $25,200. Quarter 4 payout = $25,200 Total earnings for year: $8,750 + $7,090 + $18,160 + $25,200 = $59,200

Table A-9 Commission Rate per MWH

	Cumulative MWH To Date	
Cumulative Contracts To Date	80,000–120,000	> 120,000
10–19	.08	.09
20–29	.18	.20
30–39	.29	.31
40–49	.31	.37
50+	.33	.44

Quarter	Percent Target Earnings Guaranteed	Payout Amount Guaranteed	Cumulative Payout Guaranteed
1	100%	$8,750.00	$ 8,750.00
2	75%	$6,562.50	$15,312.50
3	50%	$4,375.00	$19,687.50
4	25%	$2,187.00	$21,875.00

Figure A-6 Guranteed incentive chart.

Appendix B

Sales Compensation Surveys

Survey companies provide survey data on labor market rates for various industries. Contact the following vendors to determine if they provide the survey data to help set your target pay levels.

Table B-1 Representative Companies

Company	Web Site	Industry Focus
The Croner Company Inc.	www.croner.biz	High tech, media
Culpepper and Associates, Inc.	www.culpepper.com	Advertising, high tech, software, life sciences, telecom, IT
Hay Group, Inc.	www.haygroup.com	Pharmaceutical, credit card, insurance
Hewitt Associates, Inc.	www.hewitt.com	Various industries
McLagan Partners, Inc. (Aon)	www.mclagan.com	Financial services
Mercer Human Resource Consulting LLC	www.mercer.com	Various industries, global
ORC Worldwide	www.orcworldwide.com	Medical devices
Pearl Meyer & Partners LLC	www.pearlmeyer.com	High tech, life sciences
Radford (Aon)	www.radford.com	High tech, global
Salary.com, Inc.	www.salary.com	Various industries, global
Towers Perrin	www.towersperrin.com	Various industries, global
Watson Wyatt Worldwide, Inc.	www.watsonwyatt.com	Various industries, global
Western Management Group	www.wmgnet.com	High tech, consumer products, advertising

Software Vendors— Sales Compensation Administration Software

Software vendors providing administration solutions for sales compensation are numerous. When selecting a vendor, research the market. Companies enter and exit this space frequently. Listed below are select service providers.

Table C-1 Select Service Providers

Company	Web Site
ACTEK, Inc.	www.acteksoft.com
Callidus Software Inc.	www.callidussoftware.com
Computer Solutions & Software International (CSSI)	www.vuesoftware.com
Enterprise Incentive Software, Inc. (EI Software)	www.eimsoftware.com
Glow Teknologies, Inc.	www.glocent.com
Merced Systems	www.mercedsystems.com
nGenera Corp.	www.ngenera.com
Oracle	www.oracle.com
SAP	www.sap.com
SunGard	www.sungard.com
Synygy, Inc.	www.synygy.com
Varicent Software Inc.	www.varicent.com
Versata	www.versata.com
Xactly Corporation	www.xactlycorp.com
ZS Associates, Inc.	www.zsassociates.com

Index

About the Author

David J. Cichelli is Senior Vice President of The Alexander Group. He has been an instructor for several academic programs, including one at Columbia University. He is a frequent speaker at national association meetings and serves clients from a variety of industries, including financial services, high-tech, software, telecom, and healthcare. Cichelli authored WorldatWork's one-day class on sales compensation. He lives in Scottsdale, AZ.